LOST
ANIMALS

For Josh

© 2020 Welbeck Publishing Group Limited

All rights reserved. No part of this publication may be reproduced or transmitted in any form or by any means, electronic or mechanical, including photocopying, recording, or information storage or retrieval system, without permission in writing from the publishers.

This book may be purchased for educational, business, or sales promotional use. For information, please write: Special Markets Department, Smithsonian Books, P.O. Box 37012, MRC 513, Washington, DC 20013

Published in the United States and Canada by Smithsonian Books
Director: Carolyn Gleason
Senior Editor: Jaime Schwender
Assistant Editor: Julie Huggins

Library of Congress Cataloging-in-Publication Data

Names: Whitfield, John, 1970- author.
Title: Lost animals : extinct, endangered, and rediscovered species / John
  Whitfield.
Description: Washington, DC : Smithsonian Books, [2020] | Includes
  bibliographical references and index. | Summary: "Meet the incredible
  animals that have disappeared due to competition, mass extinctions,
  hunting, and human activity"-- Provided by publisher.
Identifiers: LCCN 2020016715 | ISBN 9781588346988 (hardcover)
Subjects: LCSH: Extinct animals. | Endangered species.
Classification: LCC QL88 .W45 2020 | DDC 591.68--dc23
LC record available at https://lccn.loc.gov/2020016715

Printed in United Arab Emirates, not at government expense
24 23 22 21 20   1 2 3 4 5

For permission to reproduce illustrations appearing in this book, please correspond directly with the owners of the works. Smithsonian Books does not retain reproduction rights for these images individually, or maintain a file of addresses for sources.

LOST ANIMALS

EXTINCT, ENDANGERED, AND REDISCOVERED SPECIES

JOHN WHITFIELD

Smithsonian Books
Washington, DC

CONTENTS

OPPOSITE: Sea scorpion fossil, *Pterygotus macrophthalmus.*

INTRODUCTION

A beautiful fossil of a horseshoe crab—and its
tracks—from the Jurassic period.

Life is more than 3.5 billion years old. Animals are about 600 million years old. _Homo sapiens_ is 300,000 years old. Recorded history is less than 10,000 years old. Humans, in other words, have seen only a tiny fraction of what Earth and life are capable of.

The world has been frozen, with the ice caps extending close to the equator. It has sweltered, with no ice at the poles and tropical forests growing where reindeer live today. Sea levels have stood more than 650 feet (200 m) higher than at present, turning continents into groups of islands. It has also been more than 320 feet (100 m) lower, creating land bridges where today there is water. The continents have come together and pulled apart again and again.

If these scenarios sound like scenes out of science-fiction stories, so do the animals that lived in them. In the past, Earth has been home to giant underwater scorpions, reptilian dolphins, saber-toothed marsupials, birds as tall as elephants, and one-ton guinea pigs, among many others.

None of these creatures is alive today. Something in their world changed—perhaps the climate shifted, or their food disappeared, or new predators or diseases arrived—and they could not adapt. Like more than 99 percent of all the species that have ever existed, they are extinct.

We know they were here because they left their fossils behind. Fossils, however, are not a perfect record of past life. Creatures that live in water are more likely to be buried than those on land. Hard parts, such as bones and shells, are better preserved than soft bodies, skin, or feathers. Older fossils are less likely to survive to the present.

Even so, fossils provide a detailed picture of Earth's past. They show that extinction is a continuous process that eventually comes to every species.

Scientists use the comings and goings of different animals to divide Earth's history into periods. Bursts of extinction become boundaries, such as between the Cambrian and Ordovician periods 488 million years ago, or between the Paleogene and Neogene periods 23 million years ago. These periods are, in turn, subdivided into epochs, and they also grouped into three eras covering the last 542 million years: the Paleozoic, Mesozoic, and Cenozoic.

During the past half-billion years, five points in time have seen particularly devastating bursts of extinction. Each of these five mass extinctions claimed three-quarters or more of all species. The largest, marking the end of the Permian period and the Paleozoic era, nearly wiped out animal life altogether.

These previous mass extinctions were all periods of rapid climate change—either cooling or warming. On one occasion, a huge rock from space smashed into Earth, blotting out the sun with smoke and dust and poisoning the air and water. That impact, 66 million years ago, brought about the end of the dinosaurs and the Mesozoic era.

But one species' catastrophe is another's opportunity. Extinction creates space for something new. Evolution causes species to change, with natural selection favoring some attributes and eliminating others. Evolution also causes species to divide. Two groups of animals living on different islands, or separated by a mountain range, will eventually become two new species.

OPPOSITE: Origins and extinctions mark the boundaries of geological time.

LIFE ON EARTH

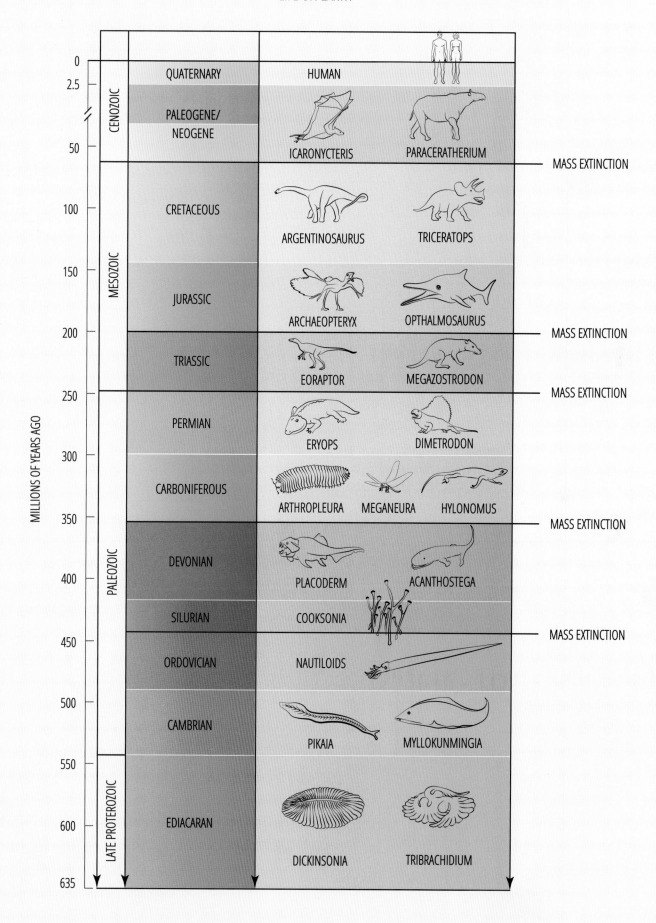

MILLIONS OF YEARS AGO

CENOZOIC	QUATERNARY	HUMAN
	PALEOGENE/ NEOGENE	ICARONYCTERIS · PARACERATHERIUM
MESOZOIC	CRETACEOUS	ARGENTINOSAURUS · TRICERATOPS
	JURASSIC	ARCHAEOPTERYX · OPTHALMOSAURUS
	TRIASSIC	EORAPTOR · MEGAZOSTRODON
PALEOZOIC	PERMIAN	ERYOPS · DIMETRODON
	CARBONIFEROUS	ARTHROPLEURA · MEGANEURA · HYLONOMUS
	DEVONIAN	PLACODERM · ACANTHOSTEGA
	SILURIAN	COOKSONIA
	ORDOVICIAN	NAUTILOIDS
	CAMBRIAN	PIKAIA · MYLLOKUNMINGIA
LATE PROTEROZOIC	EDIACARAN	DICKINSONIA · TRIBRACHIDIUM

0
2.5
50
100
150
200
250
300
350
400
450
500
550
600
635

MASS EXTINCTION
MASS EXTINCTION
MASS EXTINCTION
MASS EXTINCTION
MASS EXTINCTION

All these changes are visible in the fossil record. We can see animals evolving new adaptations, such as shells, legs, jaws, or wings. And we can see them separating as continents break up and seas open and close. Sometimes, as with the early bird *Archaeopteryx*, a single fossil can reveal the links between one group of animals and its ancestors.

In the last forty years, scientists have opened another window into the history of life. When genes—the DNA molecules that contain each organism's unique set of information and instructions—pass from parent to offspring, they carry with them a record of the past.

The genetic differences between species and individuals show how closely they are related, and also the point when their histories divided. The more distantly related they are, the more different their DNA will be. DNA evidence has shown us, for example, that humans are more closely related to chimpanzees than to any other great ape, and that hippos are the whales' closest living relative on land.

We can now recover DNA from remains hundreds of thousands of years old. This has revealed new information about the past, such as showing that modern humans and Neanderthals bred with one another. It has also led some to hope that extinct species, from woolly mammoths to passenger pigeons, might be resurrected.

In these pages, we'll meet extinct animals from five stretches of Earth's history. Beginning with the earliest known animals, we'll see them spread through the sea, onto land, and into the sky. We'll look at turning points in evolution and encounter some of the most spectacular creatures that ever lived. We'll meet the distant ancestors of today's animals, along with the not-so-distant ancestors of our own species.

Finally, we'll come to the present day to see how human activity is threatening to cause a sixth mass extinction and to look at some of the things we are trying to do to prevent it. If carbon emissions and global warming continue on their current paths, the next century or two could see changes so rapid and extreme that the scars they leave on nature will take tens of millions of years to heal.

It's not too late to change course, but the alarm bells are ringing loudly. We risk receiving an unpleasant lesson in just how different the world can be from the one we thought we knew.

ABOVE: The largest mass extinction ended the 300-million-year history of trilobites.

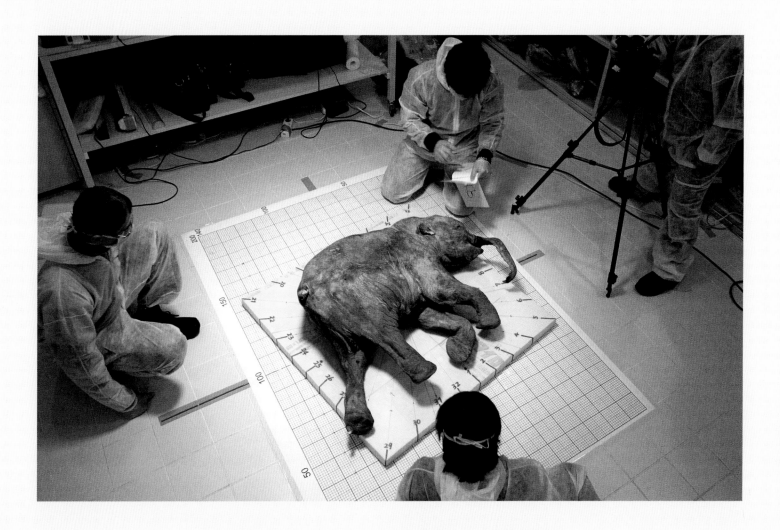

ABOVE: Scientists study the remains of a 40,000-year-old woolly mammoth calf.

FOLLOWING PAGES: Herbivores gather at a water hole on the African savanna.

FOSSIL FORMATION

A dead animal sinks in water

Its body is buried in sediment

The sediment turns to stone, and minerals replace the animal's tissues

Erosion or excavation brings the fossil to the surface

1
EARLY
ANIMALS

OPPOSITE: The animals of the Ediacaran period included *Dickinsonia* (left),
Charnia (center), and *Tribrachidium* (bottom right).

The oldest animal fossils look strange to us. It is difficult to spot similarities with creatures that evolved later. Many are shaped like fronds, mats, or disks, lacking limbs, mouths, or eyes. Which are the ancestors of snails, insects, fish, and mammals? Which were experiments in evolution that turned out to be dead ends?

The first period in the history of animals is called the Ediacaran, after the Ediacara Hills of South Australia, where some of the best-preserved fossils from this time have been found. These animals lived in the seas around Rodinia, an ancient supercontinent that was formed when the Earth's landmasses came together about a billion years ago and began to break up around 750 to 650 million years ago. They would have fed on the bacteria and other microbes raining down through the water and growing in mats on the seabed.

The Ediacaran followed an extraordinary period commonly called "Snowball Earth." About 715 million years ago, the world froze. Glaciers spread from the poles into the tropics. This big freeze was the result of a drop in atmospheric carbon dioxide. It lasted more than 100 million years, ending when volcanoes added enough carbon dioxide to the atmosphere to create a greenhouse effect that caused the ice to melt.

Ediacaran animals were completely soft-bodied creatures. Their lack of bones or shells meant that they probably would not fossilize. To be preserved, their soft body parts had

OPPOSITE: Snowball Earth, when ice covered almost the entire planet.

EARLY ANIMALS

16

THE POSITION OF THE CONTINENTS IN THE CAMBRIAN PERIOD

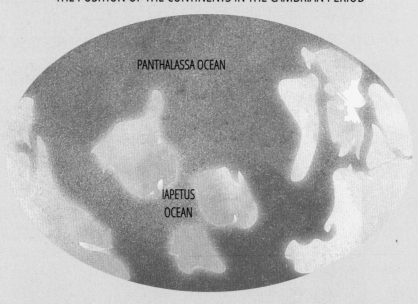

PANTHALASSA OCEAN

IAPETUS
OCEAN

to be buried quickly (in a mudslide, for example, or in a fall of volcanic ash), hidden from scavengers and cut off from oxygen. Even so, there are enough Ediacaran fossils to show that the seas were busy with animal life 550 million years ago.

About 541 million years ago, however, the Ediacaran animals were swept away. In the space of a few million years, a burst of evolution called the Cambrian explosion saw the origin of all the major animal groups alive today. It might be the most significant period in the history of animal life.

The Cambrian explosion was caused by some combination of changes to the environment and changes within animals themselves. A rise in the amount of oxygen in the sea, for example, might have been enough to enable animals to become more active, and therefore to start preying on one another. This would have spurred the origin of defenses, such as shells and burrowing, both of which appear around this time. These defenses would have prompted counterattacks by predators, such as better eyesight and sharper teeth, and so on, with each turn of the wheel increasing the complexity and diversity of animal life.

Much of what we know about the Cambrian comes from a few sites where soft-bodied animals were preserved. The most famous of these is the Burgess Shale in the Canadian Rockies. About 505 million years ago, this site was 500 feet (150 m) below the sea, at the base of a steep underwater slope. Over millennia, mudslides poured down the slope, burying the animals living at the bottom in conditions that preserved their soft body parts. The result has been a treasure trove of Cambrian life that is still yielding new discoveries to this day.

Many Cambrian animals, such as *Hallucigenia*, or the five-eyed *Opabinia*, look as strange as their Ediacaran predecessors. But unlike them, we know that they belong to groups with a long history and that have a clear place on the tree of life. By the end of the Cambrian, all the major animal groups and body plans—including the forms that would lead to vertebrates, such as ourselves—were present. The stage was set for animal life as we know it.

OPPOSITE: Canada's Burgess Shale holds one of the best records of the Cambrian explosion.

RIGHT: Fossils from the Burgess Shale of *Marrella* (left) and *Burgessia*.

Dickinsonia

PERIOD: Ediacaran
LOCALITY: Australia, Russia
SIZE: 3 ft. 3 in. (1 m) long

*D*ickinsonia, which lived in the sea about 560 million years ago, is a contender for being the most ancient animal we have yet discovered. At this time, all animals had a soft body, so they fossilized only in special conditions. As well as being one of the oldest known animals, *Dickinsonia* is one of the most common fossils found in Ediacaran rocks, with nine different species currently recognized.

Dickinsonia was oval and covered in ridges formed by its segmented body. It could reach up to 4 feet 6 inches (1.4 m) long but only grew a fraction of an inch thick—the largest fossils resemble a frilly rug. For many years, scientists debated whether it was an animal, plant, or fungus. In 2018 a team working in Australia settled the question by detecting traces of fatty chemicals in its fossils that are unique to multicellular animals. Another clue that *Dickinsonia* was an animal is that when several fossils are found, they often point in different directions, showing that it did not simply drift on the current but could crawl along in search of its food like a worm, perhaps grazing on microscopic life. It's difficult to know what and how it ate, because fossils show no trace of a mouth or digestive tract.

Even though we are learning an increasing amount about Ediacaran life, we may never be sure where species such as *Dickinsonia* belong on the animals' family tree. Is it, for example, related to jellyfish and sea anemones? Is it a giant flattened worm? Or did it leave no descendants and therefore has no relatives that are alive today? The same is true for most other Ediacaran species, which look radically different from anything that appeared after them.

LEFT: A paleontologist studies fossils of *Dickinsonia* in the Ediacara Hills of South Australia.

Charnia

PERIOD: Ediacaran
LOCALITY: Europe, Australia, Canada
SIZE: 8 in.–6 ft. 6 in. (20 cm–2 m) long

In April 1957, three English schoolchildren were on a rock-climbing trip to a quarry in Charnwood Forest in Leicestershire, England. They found a leaflike fossil; one of them, Roger Mason, showed it to his father, who brought it to a geologist at the local university. Now known as *Charnia masoni*, it was the first discovery of an animal from before the Cambrian Period. Since then, fossils of *Charnia masoni* have been found at more locations, in rocks formed over a greater span of time, than any other animal that lived so long ago.

With its fernlike fronds, *Charnia* might look like a plant; however, the rocks in which it is found show that it lived in deep water where it would have been too dark for plants to grow. We cannot tell whether or how it is related to any animal alive today. Since its discovery, it has been found at sites in Canada, Russia, and Australia in rocks formed from sand, mud, or volcanic ash that range from 575 million to about 550 million years old. Along with *Dickinsonia*, this makes *Charnia* another contender for the oldest known animal.

Charnia had a soft body, lacking a skeleton or shell. Most fossils are about 8 inches (20 cm) long, although a related species found in Canada, *Charnia wardi*, grew to 6 feet 6 inches (2 m), making it the longest animal of its period. *Charnia* rooted itself to the seabed with a disk or holdfast and grew as a frond on its stalk. There is no sign of any mouth or digestive tract, but it probably fed by either filtering or absorbing food from the water.

RIGHT: *Charnia* had a fernlike body and a stalk that attached to the seabed.

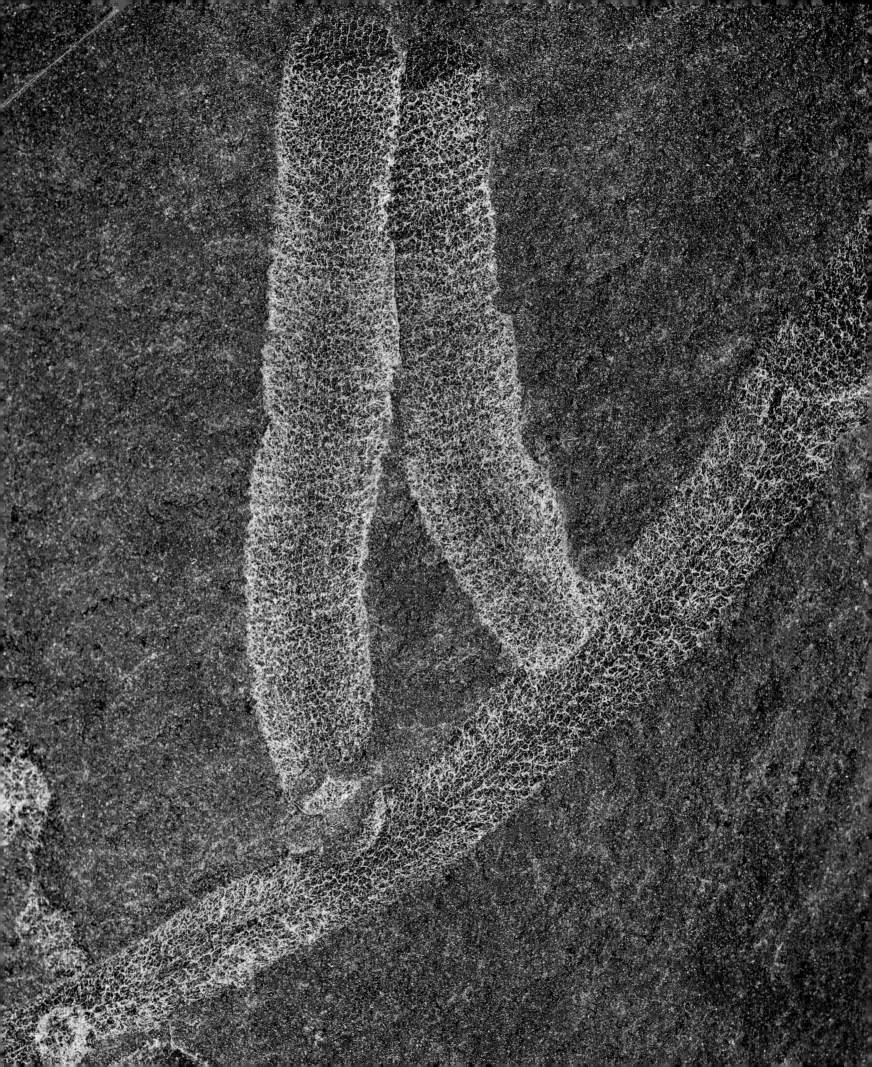

CLASSIFICATION: Porifera
LOCALITY: Australia, Africa, China
PERIOD: Cryogenian–Ediacaran
SIZE: Microscopic to $^1/_{32}$ in. (1 mm)

Sponges

200 μm

Sponges are arguably the simplest animals alive today, lacking organs, muscles, and nerves. They root themselves to the seafloor and take in water through the holes in their bodies, straining out microscopic pieces of food.

Comparing the DNA of living sponges with that of other animals shows that the sponges' branch split from the rest of the family tree over 700 million years ago. There are chemical traces in rocks of a similar age that some believe are the remains of sponges, although not all scientists agree. The oldest candidate fossils that we know of come from Namibia and Australia, dating from about 650 million years ago, but again, experts disagree over whether these are true sponges. In 2015 Chinese researchers unveiled the best-preserved Precambrian fossil sponge, a tiny animal about $^1/_{32}$ inch (1 mm) across, christened *Eocyathispongia qiania*. It dates from 600 million years ago and was discovered in the Doushantuo Formation at Weng'an phosphate mining area in southwest China, a site that has yielded many spectacular fossils of ancient soft-bodied creatures.

Fossil sponges are common from the Cambrian period onward, but they are rare before it. This is puzzling, because the bodies of modern sponges are made up of mineral building blocks like intricate crystals or snowflakes. It would be wrong to call this a skeleton—sponges are less structured than other animals—but these spicules, as they are called, should still be preserved in the rocks.

One line of thought is that sponges evolved mineral spicules only in the Cambrian period, 540 million years ago, and that before this their spicules were fleshy and therefore probably did not fossilize. This theory is supported by fossils from the early Cambrian period that appear to show sponges on their way to developing a mineral frame.

Whatever happened in their early history, sponges were common in the Cambrian seas. They also changed the world for other species, because they were the first known reef-building animals. From about 525 million years ago, sponges grew into huge structures that, like today's corals, would have provided homes for countless other creatures. Rocks in northern Siberia contain the remains of what must have been spectacular reefs, stretching for more than 900 miles (1,500 km) and more than 120 miles (200 km) across.

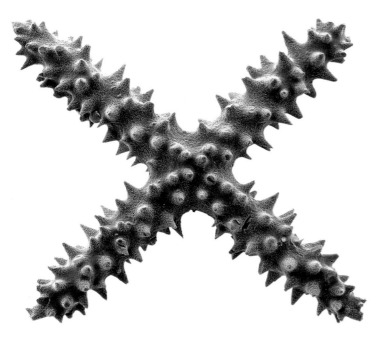

OPPOSITE: *Vauxia gracilenta*, a fossil sponge from the Cambrian period.

ABOVE: *Eocyathispongia qiania*, a tiny, 600-million-year-old fossil sponge from China.

LEFT: Sponges have a simple skeleton made up of microscopic mineral structures called spicules.

23

Kimberella and Tribrachidium

KIMBERELLA
PERIOD: Ediacaran
LOCALITY: Australia, Russia
SIZE: 6 in. (15 cm) long,
2 in. (5 cm) wide

TRIBRACHIDIUM
PERIOD: Ediacaran
LOCALITY: Australia, Russia
SIZE: 1½ in. (4 cm) across

Nearly every living animal has front and back ends that are different, as well as left and right sides that mirror each other. This is a good body plan for a mobile lifestyle; your eyes and mouth can point in the direction you are going, while at the other end, you leave your waste behind you. Matching left and right sides enable the body to develop features that work well in pairs, such as eyes, antennae, or legs.

This body plan is known as bilateral symmetry, and *Kimberella* is the oldest known example of it. It was discovered in the 1940s in 555-million-year-old rocks among the Ediacara Hills in Australia.

The animal grew up to 6 inches (15 cm) long, 2 inches (5 cm) wide, and about 1½ inches (4 cm) high. It had a single, wide muscly foot for moving around, a tough but flexible shell it could pull its soft body into when threatened, and hard teeth that were probably used for scraping food off the rocks. We know this because some of the rocks that contain fossil *Kimberella* also preserve traces of its tracks and teeth marks.

All these features—the muscly foot, scraping teeth, and a shell to hide in—are today found in snails, which belong to a large and successful group of animals called the mollusks. *Kimberella* is an obvious candidate for the oldest known mollusk, or perhaps their relative or ancestor, although debate continues about exactly how the animal looked and lived, and where it belongs on the tree of life.

Today animals with two-fold symmetry like *Kimberella*'s can be seen everywhere. Conversely, bodies built with threefold symmetry are nonexistent. But long ago in the early history of animals, there were creatures with bodies divided into three rather than two.

Tribrachidium was one such animal. It lived on the seabed in shallow waters 550 million years ago. It could reach up to 1½ inches (4 cm) across, although most fossils are much smaller, with a hemispheric body rising a fraction of an inch above the seabed.

On top of its body were three ridges, beginning in its center and curving away to the edges. These grooves would have created eddies that directed water into the three pits on the upper surface of the animal, enabling any tiny food particles to be extracted.

This form of feeding would have effectively cleaned the water, making it clearer and richer in oxygen—perhaps helping to create conditions that favored the evolution of both more mobile, energy-hungry animals and the development of eyes.

This type of body seems to have been an experiment that evolution abandoned early in the history of animals. Researchers have suggested that the closest living relatives of *Tribrachidium* could be either sea anemones or starfish.

ABOVE: *Kimberella* fossil from the White Sea, Russia. The animal had a muscly foot, tough shell, and hard teeth like a snail.

OPPOSITE: *Tribrachidium* is the only known animal with a body plan divided into three.

Cloudina

Building a shell takes a great deal of effort—effort that could otherwise be used elsewhere, such as growing a larger body or producing more offspring. It's worth the investment only if it's really needed—in other words, if the alternative is being eaten.

The first animals were not predators. They lacked jaws and—as far as we can tell from the fossil record—mouths. They moved slowly, if at all. But at some point animals evolved the ability to eat other animals, and from that point onward, any potential prey needed to be able to defend itself.

Cloudina is the first animal known to have had what is technically known as a mineralized exoskeleton: a shell. It lived toward the end of the Ediacaran period, about 540 million years ago, and seems to have been widespread. Fossils have been found in Africa, Asia, North and South America, Europe, and Antarctica in limestone rocks formed from large growths of microorganisms called stromatolites.

The shell built by *Cloudina* comprised open-ended cones stacked inside one another, creating a tube for the animal to live in. The longest examples are 6 inches (15 cm) long and about ¼ inch (6 mm) across. Exactly how *Cloudina* lived—what it fed on and whether it burrowed into the seabed or rested on top of it—remains elusive.

Proof that *Cloudina* needed protection is shown by the holes bored into some fossil shells. These were almost certainly made by a predator trying to get at the creature inside. This is the oldest evidence we have of one animal trying to eat another. It sets the stage for the great battles between predators and their prey, one of the most significant factors in evolution, and one of the driving forces behind the complexity and diversity of the animal kingdom.

27

LEFT: *Cloudina* had a tubular shell made up of many segments.

Hallucigenia

PERIOD: Cambrian
LOCALITY: Canada, China
SIZE: ¾ in. (2 cm) long

I f you had been scuba diving during the Cambrian period, it would have been easy to miss *Hallucigenia sparsa*. It was only about ¾ inch (2 cm) long and thinner than a hair. But if you had seen it, it would have been hard to forget.

Hallucigenia had a soft body, protected by hard spines on its back. Underneath, it had ten pairs of legs. The rear seven ended in claws and would have been used for walking. The front three were thinner and longer and may have been covered in fine hairs used to filter food from the water and pass it to the creature's mouth. It chewed its food with one set of teeth ringing its mouth and another set farther down its throat, and it sensed its environment with two small eyes and a pair of antennae.

Based on 508-million-year-old fossils discovered in the Burgess Shale, Canada, Simon Conway-Morris, the British paleontologist who gave *Hallucigenia* its name, thought that the animal stood on its spines and had a single row of tentacles running down its back. It turned out, however, that Conway-Morris was looking at a squashed animal, and better-preserved specimens enabled *Hallucigenia* to be reconceived. Today three species of *Hallucigenia* are known, of different sizes and with different lengths of spines, as well as related species with similar spines and legs from early in the Cambrian period.

Hallucigenia's closest living relatives are a group called the velvet worms. These look a little like a cross between a caterpillar and a centipede, although velvet worms are closely related to neither. About 200 species of velvet worms are known, all of which live on the land. This is unusual, because most of the main animal groups include some sea-dwelling species. *Hallucigenia* and its relatives suggest that the ancestors of velvet worms started out under water.

ABOVE RIGHT: Fossil of *Hallucigenia* from the Burgess Shale, Canada, showing the spines pointing down beneath the body.

RIGHT: *Hallucigenia* walked on spindly legs and had spines on its back for protection.

Wiwaxia

PERIOD: Cambrian
LOCALITY: Canada, China, Europe, Australia
SIZE: 2 in. (5 cm) long

Scientists have determined that most Cambrian animals belong to groups that are still alive today, such as arthropods—the group that includes insects and crabs—and mollusks. But *Wiwaxia* remains mysterious.

Wiwaxia corrugata grew to be about 2 inches (5 cm) long and its body probably reached about ½ inch (1 cm) tall. Two rows of spines, which could reach 2 inches (5 cm) long, grew out of its back. Together with the eight rows of armored plates that covered its body, these spines must have given *Wiwaxia* useful protection against predators. It is one of the most widespread Cambrian fossil animals; since its discovery in the Burgess Shale in Canada, it has also been found in China, Russia, Australia, and the Czech Republic.

Fossils show that some *Wiwaxia* had clam-like shelled creatures called brachiopods living attached to their backs, suggesting that it sat on the seabed instead of burrowing into it. It was probably a grazer, scraping a diet of bacteria off the ocean floor.

To back up its armor, *Wiwaxia* may have also flashed out a warning to possible predators. Microscopic structures on its scales reflect light like the shiny back of a beetle. Scientists have suggested that as the light bounced off its scales, *Wiwaxia* shimmered blue, green, and yellow, warning off attackers.

Experts disagree about where *Wiwaxia* belongs on the tree of life, because its anatomy is a strange mixture. Its scales resemble those of a group of modern sea-living worms. But its mouthparts look more like those of a snail. Some have suggested it is close to the ancestor from which both groups split, while others believe that it is neither a worm nor a mollusk and should be regarded as part of an extinct group of its own.

OPPOSITE: *Wiwaxia's* spines and scales provided a good defense against predators.

RIGHT: Fossil *Wiwaxia* from the Burgess Shale, Canada.

Pikaia and Myllokunmingia

PIKAIA
PERIOD: Cambrian
LOCALITY: Canada
SIZE: 2 in. (5 cm) long

MYLLOKUNMINGIA
PERIOD: Cambrian
LOCALITY: China
SIZE: 1 in. (2.5 cm) long

*P*ikaia gracilens wasn't particularly big, reaching only about the length of your thumb. If the fossils we have can be used as an accurate guide, it wasn't especially common. *Myllokunmingia* was even smaller, being only about the size of a paper clip.

But for humans, *Pikaia* and *Myllokunmingia* are special because they are among the earliest known species of the group to which we and all other vertebrates belong: the chordates.

Pikaia was discovered more than a century ago by American paleontologist Charles Walcott in the 508-million-year-old rocks of the Burgess Shale in the Rocky Mountains of British Columbia, Canada. It didn't have a skeleton, but it did have a notochord, a flexible rod of cells running down its body similar to a backbone. This is what gives chordates their name; it is still present in modern vertebrates' embryos, which gradually form the spine.

Pikaia had a fin on its back and could probably swim by flexing its body like an eel; it probably spent much of its time on the ocean floor. Some specimens have fossilized mud in their digestive tract, suggesting that it fed by plucking morsels off the seabed.

Pikaia also had muscles, nerves, and blood vessels characteristic of later fish, reptiles, and other animals with skeletons. But certain aspects of its form remain strange and mysterious. For example, it had a pair of long tentacles on the top of its head and several pairs of smaller appendages just beneath these on the underside of its body. These may have been gills used for breathing underwater.

Myllokunmingia fengjiaoa has been found in older rocks than *Pikaia*—dating from 530 million years ago, early in the Cambrian period—located in the Maotianshan Shales of the Chengjiang Formation in southern China. But although its fossil record reaches back farther in time than *Pikaia*'s, it is arguably more similar to a fish, showing fins, muscles, a skull, and possibly gills. Many researchers regard *Myllokunmingia*, along with other similar species also found in Chengjiang, as the first known vertebrate. However, it was not bony; instead its skeleton was made from soft cartilage.

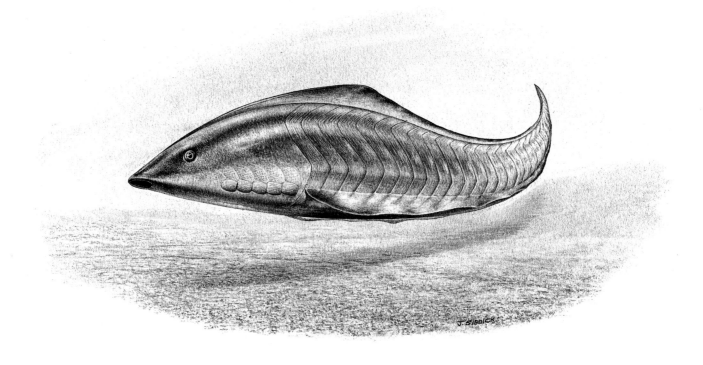

OPPOSITE: *Myllokunmingia*, found in China, is the oldest known vertebrate.

BELOW: *Pikaia* could swim by flexing its body like an eel.

Trilobites

PERIOD: Cambrian–Permian
LOCALITY: Worldwide
SIZE: Various

A tough external skeleton, with joints that enable different sections of the body to work as legs, jaws, pincers, or feelers, might have been the most significant evolutionary innovation of early animals. The phylum that possesses such a skeleton, known as arthropoda, includes insects, spiders, crabs, and centipedes—Earth's most diverse and numerous animal group.

Five hundred million years ago the most ubiquitous arthropods were the trilobites. They thrived in Cambrian seas, living in all habitats from coral reefs to the deep ocean. Most scuttled on the seabed, and probably scavenged or hunted soft food such as worms, although many were specialized for other ways of life, such as filter feeding. With their tough skeletons and compound eyes made up of hundreds or even thousands of lenses—like modern-day dragonflies—they were superbly adapted for marine life.

Trilobites' bodies were formed in segments. They were divided into three, both from side to side—the three lobes that give them their name—and from front to back. Like modern arthropods, they had discrete head, thorax, and tail sections. Among their living relatives, they are thought to be closest to spiders and scorpions.

Along its length, the trilobite's body was divided into still more segments, each of which carried a pair of attachments, such as antennae, mouthparts, or legs. This basic body plan could be modified, with the spines stretching and twisting into weird and wonderful shapes, eyes rising on stalks above the body and shells growing into pointed fronts like a lance or spatula.

Olennus gilberti shows the striking, spiny plumage that evolved early in the trilobites' history. It lived in the Cambrian period, about 520 million years ago, and was discovered in the Pioche Shale in Nevada, one of the rare sites where soft-bodied animals from this time are preserved. Spines on this and other species are thought to be defences against predators; some specimens show damaged spines in the process of regrowing.

Trilobites came in all sizes as well as shapes. The smallest was the size of a fingernail; the largest were more than 2 feet 3½ inches (70 cm) long and would have weighed as much as 10 pounds (4.5 kg). Most species, including *Olennus*, grew 1 to 4 inches (3–10 cm) long.

Trilobites lived for 270 million years, making them one of the most successful groups in the history of life. They were so common and widespread that the Paleozoic era, which ran from 540 million to 250 million years ago, is sometimes called "the Age of the Trilobites."

More than 20,000 species are known from rocks found around the world, from their appearance early in the Cambrian period to their demise at the end of the Permian period, in the largest of all mass extinctions.

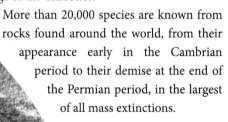

OPPOSITE: Trilobites were abundant for more than 250 million years.

RIGHT: Fossil of *Olennus gilberti*, a spiny Cambrian trilobite from North America.

Marrella

PERIOD: Cambrian
LOCALITY: Canada, China
SIZE: 1 in. (2.5 cm) long

More than 25,000 specimens of *Marrella splendens* have been excavated from the Burgess Shale, the site in the Canadian Rockies where the rocks have preserved a wonderful array of both hard- and soft-bodied creatures from more than 500 million years ago. This makes it one of the most common and best-known Cambrian fossils; here, at least, the ocean must have been teeming with these little creatures. *Marrella* is also known from China, and fossils of related species have been found in Australia.

Superficially, *Marrella* looks a little like a crustacean—when he discovered it in 1910, Charles Walcott described it in his notebook as a "lace crab"—and a little like a trilobite, but its exact relationship to the other arthropods is uncertain.

Marrella had two long pairs of spines on the top of its head and two pairs of mobile appendages growing lower down from each side of its head. One of these lower pairs were long, delicate antennae used for feeling its way as it moved over the seabed. The other pair were much more robust and covered in fine hairs, suggesting that they were paddles that propelled the animal forward with each sweep. *Marrella* probably used a mixture of hunting and scavenging to feed, perhaps using its legs—which bear fine, hairlike projections—to strain food out of the water as it swam.

The largest known *Marrella* fossils are just under 1 inch (2.5 cm) long. *Marrella* has been found fossilized in the process of molting, shedding its tough exoskeleton so that its body could grow larger before its soft exterior hardened again. This is the oldest known fossil record of molting, which is still used by all modern arthropods.

OPPOSITE: *Marrella* had many different appendages for feeding and swimming.

ABOVE: *Marrella* is one of the most common fossils in the Burgess Shale.

Nectocaris

O ctopus and squid are among the most sophisticated and dominant animals in the sea, being nimble, fast-moving, and more intelligent than any other invertebrate. Hundreds of species are known, some of them capable of growing to a huge size. They are mollusks and belong to a group called the cephalopods.

The earliest cephalopod fossils date from near the end of the Cambrian period, about 500 million years ago. We know these fossils are the remains of cephalopods instead of slow-moving, bottom-dwelling snails, because their shells contain gas-filled chambers that would have helped the animal float in the water, enabling it to swim. Modern octopus and squid have lost these shells, but one group of modern cephalopods, called nautiloids, still have them.

In 2010 scientists studying Canadian fossils sought to push back the cephalopod fossil record by 10 million years, into the early Cambrian. They argued that *Nectocaris pteryx*, a 2- to 3-inch (5-cm) creature that was previously thought to be either an arthropod or a chordate, was the earliest known cephalopod.

This conclusion was based on evidence that *Nectocaris* had good eyesight (like modern squid and octopus) and a pair of long, flexible tentacles near its mouth. Most significantly, it had a structure behind its eyes that, the researchers argued, was the remains of a tubular structure called a siphon. Cephalopods are the only animals to have siphons; by squirting water from them, they can gain a sudden burst of speed, making them the only animals to have a built-in jet engine.

Not everyone agrees with this interpretation, and whether *Nectocaris* was really a mollusk is still controversial. What's more certain is that cephalopods evolved rapidly in the late Cambrian, with more than 140 species known.

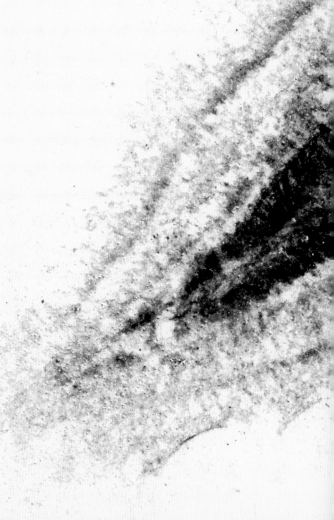

RIGHT: Some scientists believe *Nectocaris* is the earliest member of the group containing squid and octopus.

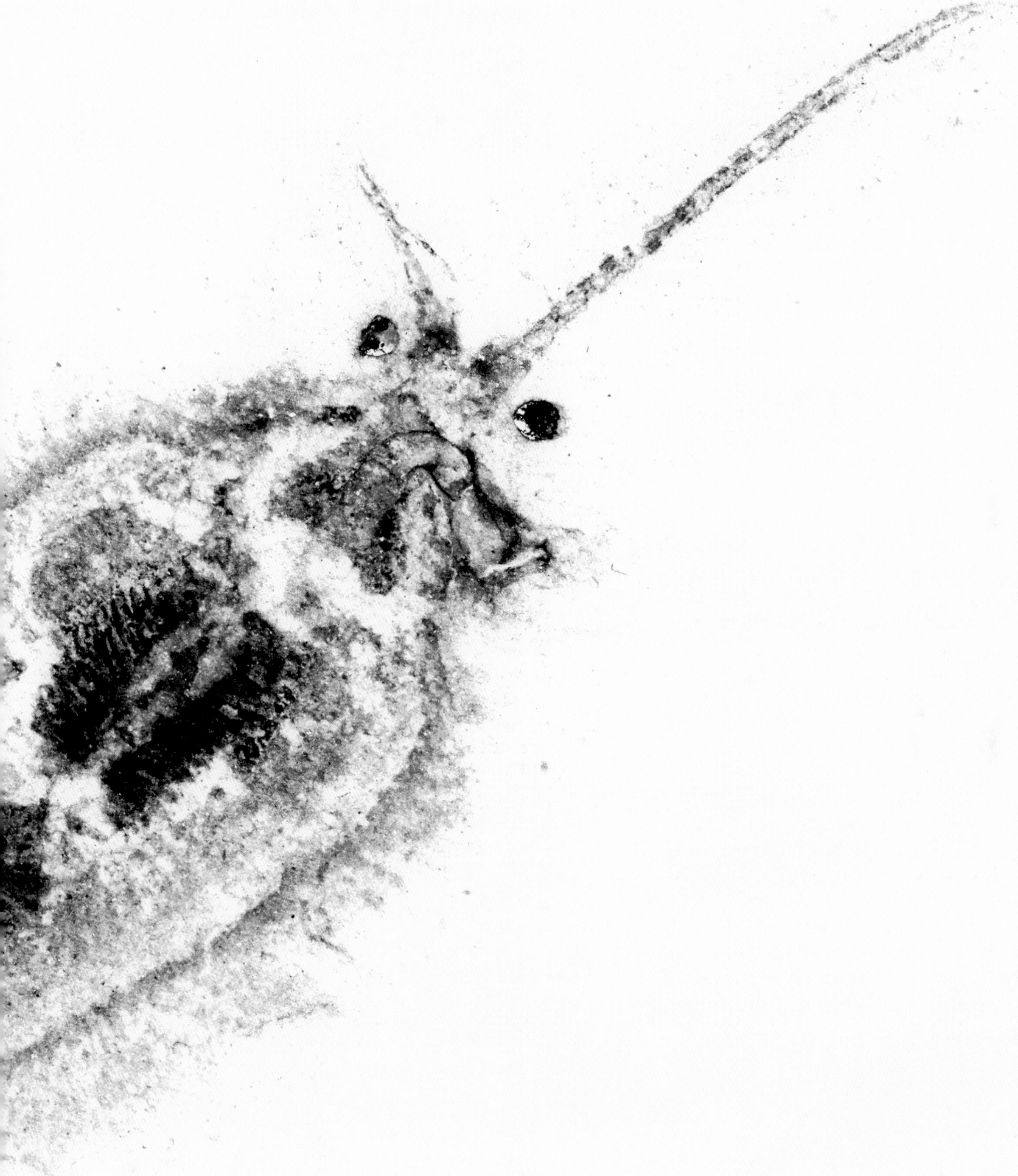

Opabinia and Anomalocaris

OPABINIA
PERIOD: Cambrian
LOCALITY: Canada
Size: 2 in. (5 cm) long

ANOMALOCARIS
PERIOD: Cambrian
LOCALITY: Canada, China, Australia
SIZE: 3 ft. 3 in. (1 m) long

A shrimplike body. Five eyes. A trunk. No legs. No wonder that when a reconstruction of *Opabinia regalis* was unveiled at a scientific meeting in the 1970s, the audience burst out laughing.

Short stalks supported *Opabinia*'s eyes, giving them the appearance of protruding mushrooms. There was a pair at the front, a pair at the back, and one in the middle, pointing upward. Its flexible proboscis hung beneath its head and was tipped with a clawed, spiny grabber, which was presumably used to pass food into its mouth. It was located beneath its body and pointed backward, so it must have eaten like an elephant snacking on peanuts. It lacked powerful jaws, so it probably ate soft food, perhaps using its proboscis to drag worms out of their burrows, for example.

Although *Opabinia* didn't have legs, the fifteen segments of its body were fringed with jointed flaps, which could have helped it crawl or swim. These flaps also contained the animal's gills. Its fanned tail, a little like a lobster's, could have been used to help it move and steer.

For a while, many regarded *Opabinia* as a weird unique creature—a body form that had evolved in the Cambrian but left no descendants among later species. But careful comparisons of many species, both living and fossil, have led researchers to think that it is related to other soft-bodied, segmented animals, and it may be a distant relation of the arthropods.

The yard-long *Anomalocaris* was another member of this group. It got its name, which means "weird shrimp," because scientists mistook its tough mouthparts, which fossilize much more easily than its soft body, to be the remains of shrimp. Other parts of its body have been variously misidentified as belonging to a crustacean, a sea cucumber, and a jellyfish. It took decades of research before scientists realized that all these parts belonged to a single animal, the largest known from the Cambrian.

Anomalocaris was a fearsome hunter, the top predator in the Cambrian seas. Armed with spines, its mouthparts hung down ready to grab food and sweep it into the animal's mouth, where it could be crunched up. Its compound eyes were as good as any insect's, each ¾ inch (2 cm) across and comprising up to 16,000 lenses. The favorite prey of *Anomalocaris* may have been trilobites; bite marks have been found on trilobite fossils that match its jaws.

A few dozen species of anomalocarids have been found in rocks dating to the Cambrian period from Greenland to Australia. The shape of the mouthparts varies from species to species, suggesting that they ate different foods. Some seem to have been specialized for grabbing prey; others may have grubbed in the muddy seabed or strained the water for tiny creatures.

Even after fish evolved, anomalocarids continued to be some of the biggest animals on Earth. In 2015 researchers discovered that one species survived into the geological period following the Cambrian: the Ordovician. This creature, called *Aegirocassis*, really made its Cambrian relatives look like shrimp; growing to about 6 feet 6 inches (2 m) long, it cruised the oceans filtering plankton.

OPPOSITE: The bizarre-looking *Opabinia* is a distant relative of insects and crustaceans.

RIGHT AND FOLLOWING PAGES: With spiny mouthparts and excellent eyes, *Anomalocaris* was the biggest, fiercest creature in the Cambrian seas.

2
ONTO LAND

OPPOSITE: The forests of the Carboniferous period were home
to giant invertebrates such as the dragonfly *Meganeura*.

PERIOD

ORDOVICIAN (485–444 million years ago)
SILURIAN (444–419 million years ago)
DEVONIAN (419–359 million years ago)
CARBONIFEROUS (359–299 million years ago)
PERMIAN (299–251 million years ago)

At the beginning of the Ordovician period, 485 million years ago, the diversity of animals exploded once again. In 10 million years, the number of animal species living in the sea tripled.

Fossils show more species living in deep water, more plankton feeders swimming in the open sea, and more predators adapted to catch them. Reefs built up by sponges and other creatures became larger and more widespread, creating homes and food for more animals.

Meanwhile animals were slowly venturing onto land, making brief trips out of the water and leaving their traces along the shoreline. As time passed, tracks became more common. The oldest fossils of land animals, creatures similar to centipedes and spiders, date from around 414 million years ago, toward the end of the end of the Silurian Period.

Ancient plants such as mosses were growing by this time. By the end of the next period, the Devonian, 358 million years ago, the first forests appeared, made up of fernlike plants growing more than 60 feet (20 m) high. The following period, the Carboniferous, saw swampy tropical forests filled with horsetails, tree ferns, club mosses, and conifers. Giant insects buzzed among the trees, and amphibians and small reptiles hunted or were hunted by them.

THE POSITION OF THE CONTINENTS IN THE SILURIAN PERIOD

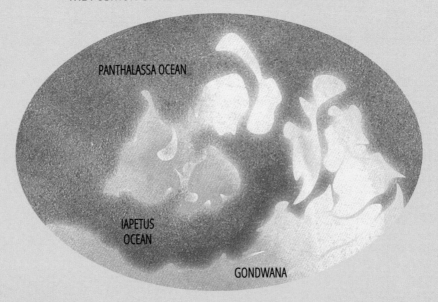

PANTHALASSA OCEAN

IAPETUS
OCEAN

GONDWANA

OPPOSITE: Many species of jawless fish, such as *Doryaspis*, lived in the Devonian oceans.

In the next period, the Permian, all the continents came together into a single landmass called Pangaea. By then, large vertebrates were common, with plant eaters the size of a rhinoceros and predators big enough to hunt them.

But if this sounds like smooth, uninterrupted progress, think again. These periods also witnessed three of the most severe mass extinctions in Earth's history.

The first came at the end of the Ordovician. Around 460 million years ago, the supercontinent Gondwana moved toward the South Pole. This shift triggered a 20-million-year-long ice age that caused a 165-foot (50-m) drop in sea levels, drying out the shallow seas in which life had thrived. The end of the Ordovician saw the second largest mass extinction in Earth's history, with a loss of 86 percent of all species.

The end of the Devonian saw another mass extinction, wiping out 75 percent of all species. Again, this collapse seems to have been partly due to an ice age causing sea levels to drop.

Most dramatic of all, the mass extinction at the end of the Permian period, 251 million years ago, saw the disappearance of 96 percent of all living species. In the sea, the trilobites, which had thrived for 250 million years, vanished completely. On the land, the forests died along with two-thirds of vertebrates. Insects experienced their only mass extinction.

The end of the Permian saw global warming. Enormous volcanic eruptions in Siberia covered an area the size of Western Europe in lava up to 2 miles (3 km) deep and released more carbon dioxide than is contained in all the world's fossil fuel deposits. These eruptions triggered a runaway greenhouse effect. The land and sea warmed by 18–27°F (10–15°C), reaching 104°F (40°C) at the equator. The rain and sea turned acid.

Before the end of the Permian, the world's ecosystems were as complex as today's. Afterward the sea was dominated by single-cell life and a few clam-like species of shelled animal. It took 100 million years until the number of species returned to the same level. It's the closest life has ever come to being completely wiped out.

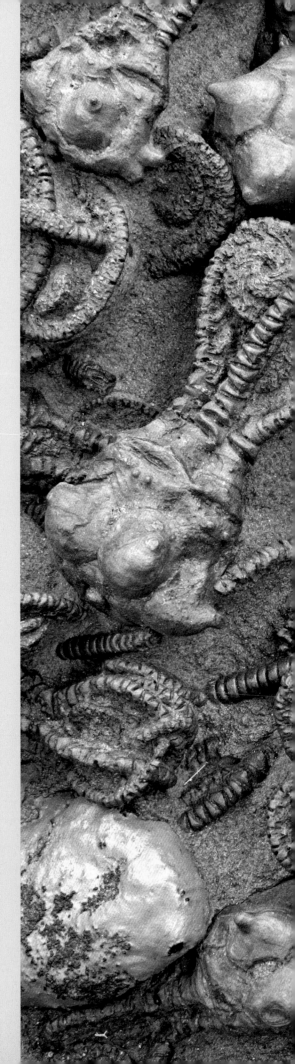

LEFT: A fossil fern from the Carboniferous period.

RIGHT: Fossil crinoids, related to starfish, from the Permian period.

Nautiloids

PERIOD: Cambrian–present
LOCALITY: Worldwide
SIZE: Various

Many of the earliest known animals lived in shallow seas close to the shore. But for any animal able to swim strongly enough, the open ocean offered a vast new territory with new sources of food and perhaps fewer predators. The nautiloids—the swimming mollusks with shells and tentacles related to squid and octopus—were one of the first groups, along with crustaceans and other arthropods, to make full use of the open sea. The fossil record of rocks from the Ordovician period, 470 million years ago, shows that nautiloids were living around the world, and that they and other animals evolved to live in deeper water.

It's thought that the first nautiloids were slow-moving plankton feeders, rising and falling in the water by moving gas in and out of the hollow chambers in their shells. They accomplished this by changing the chemical concentration of their body fluids. Increasing the concentration causes water to move out of the shell into the body, leaving gas behind. When the amount of gas in the shell goes up, so does the animal, and vice versa. This up-and-down movement is known as vertical migration, and it is a strategy still used by many of today's marine animals, which can stay at greater depths during the day to avoid predators and then rise at night to feed.

In the Ordovician, nautiloids evolved to become more mobile, able to move by blasting a jet of water out of a hole close their heads. They hunted by grabbing food with their tentacles and dragging it to their hard, beak-like mouths. Most were relatively small, with shells about 4 inches (10 cm) in length, but some were huge, with shells as long as 20 feet (6 m).

At this time, nautiloids were the top predators in the sea; damage to fossil shells shows that they probably attacked one another. Traces of color preserved on some fossils suggests that at least some species had camouflage. A darker pattern of gray and brown stripes on the upper half of these shells helped the animal blend into the dark water to anything looking down from above, while a lighter white or cream underside hid it from anything looking from underneath.

OPPOSITE: Nautiloids, one shown here attacking a trilobite, were dominant predators.

ABOVE: A fossil nautiloid shell found in England.

LEFT: A spiral-shell nautiloid fossil from the United States.

Euthycarcinoids

PERIOD: Cambrian–Triassic
LOCALITY: North America, South America, Australia
SIZE: 4 in. (10 cm)

Hundreds of millions of years ago, before seaweed or any other complex plant species had evolved, the shoreline was covered in mats of bacteria and other microbes. Any animal that could reach them at low tide could enjoy an easy meal. The risk of a meal being interrupted by a predator was also much lower out of the water than in it. From the Cambrian period onward, rocks that would have lined the water's edge bear fossilized track marks, originally made in wet sand and mud that preserved these imprints as it formed rock. These are the earliest traces of animals that had begun to make brief trips out of the water.

Euthycarcinoids are often suggested as the first animals to have made the journey from water to land. They were arthropods with an external skeleton, a jointed body with up to twenty-eight pairs of legs, and a spiny tail. They looked somewhat like a cross between a lobster and a wood louse and were the size of a large shrimp.

The rocks that contain the oldest known euthycarcinoid fossils date from the late Cambrian period, about 500 million years ago. The track marks in these rocks look as if they were made by a creature with a number of similar-size legs dragging a tail behind it—in other words, something remarkably like a euthycarcinoid.

More than a dozen species of euthycarcinoid are known, most from the much later Carboniferous period, about 350 million years ago. The oldest Cambrian species were marine animals, but those from later periods have been found at sites that were either estuaries or freshwater rivers and streams, evidence that they lived at the water's edge. They survived for more than 250 million years, into the Triassic period, before becoming extinct.

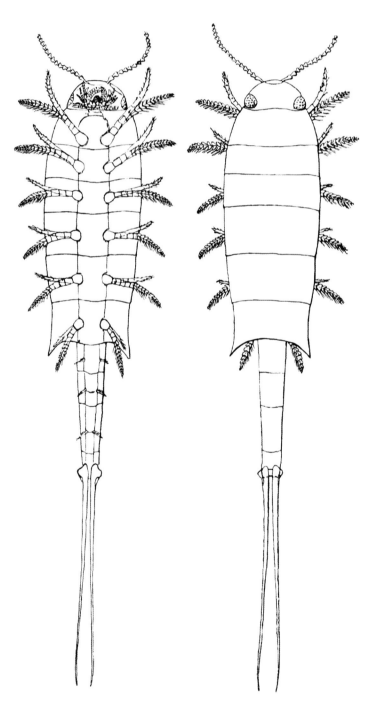

RIGHT: Euthycarcinoids may have been the first animals to venture onto land.

Sacabambaspis

PERIOD: Ordovician
LOCALITY: South America, Australia, Arabia
SIZE: 10 in. (25 cm)

Imagine a giant tadpole, and you'll have a good idea of what the first vertebrates looked like.

Sacabambaspis janvieri is one of the earliest and best-known of these first vertebrates—it's often cited as the oldest known animal to have a full skeleton. Growing to about 10 inches (25 cm) long, its most striking feature was its armored head, with bony shields on its upper and lower surfaces. These would have protected it from predators such as the large and fierce nautiloids and eurypterids.

Its fossils are known from Bolivia, Argentina, central Australia, and Oman. During the Ordovician, the world's landmasses were joined together into a supercontinent in the southern hemisphere called Gondwana. *Sacabambaspis* and other related species of early vertebrates lived in shallow water close to the shore—some fossils show scrapes on the undersides of their bodies from where they hugged the seabed.

Sacabambaspis, along with other early vertebrates, lacked jaws. It would have been a bottom-feeder, sucking or scooping food into its mouth and breaking it up by sucking and squeezing in its throat.

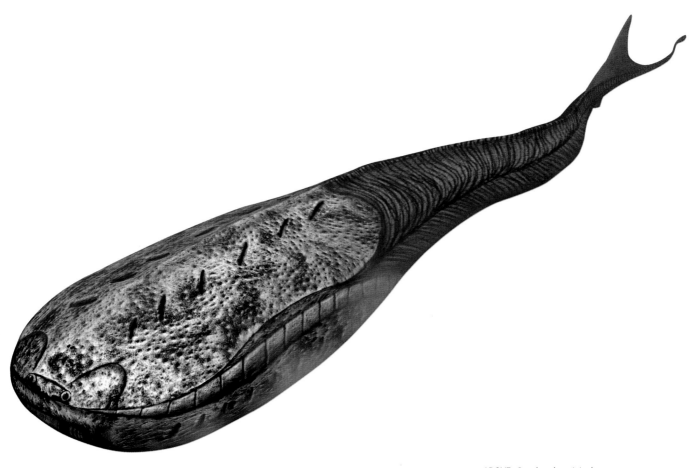

ABOVE: *Sacabambaspis* is the oldest animal with a full skeleton.

ABOVE: Eurypterids are also known as sea scorpions.

OPPOSITE: Nineteenth-century drawings of two eurypterid species: *Pterygotus bilobus* (left) and *Eurypterus remipes* (center and right).

Pterygotus

PERIOD: Ordovician–Devonian
LOCALITY: Australia, Europe, North America, South America
SIZE: 5 ft. (1.5 m) long

Today the biggest animals in the sea are vertebrates—whale and sharks—although some of the largest squid run close. But hundreds of millions of years ago, enormous invertebrates ruled the seas.

Pterygotus anglicus was one them. Its name means "winged fish," because the Swiss naturalist Louis Agassiz, who first described it in 1839, thought he was studying the remains of a large fish, not an enormous invertebrate. It belongs to an extinct group of arthropods sometimes called the sea scorpions, which are distantly related to land-dwelling scorpions.

With a body that grew to more than 5 feet (1.5 m) long, *Pterygotus anglicus* was one of several related species of giant eurypterid. Other species were smaller, at about 1 foot 6 inches (50 cm). Most lived in shallow seas, but some swam well enough to cross the ancient oceans. We know this from their worldwide distribution and because they appeared about the same time in places that were separated by thousands of miles of ocean, such as present-day Scotland and China.

Eurypterids appear in the fossil record in the Ordovician period, 470 million years ago, and survived for more than 200 million years. The greatest number of species thrived during the Silurian and Devonian periods, 400 million to 300 million years ago.

Like scorpions, *Pterygotus* and other eurypterids had a powerful pair of claws, with spiky inner surfaces ideal for gripping, killing, and tearing prey before passing it to their mouth. Combined with its good eyesight and a body built for swimming, eurypterids must have been awesome predators and an easy match for the early fish of the era. Only the claws had a bony external skeleton, meaning that fossils of these are found much more frequently than those of the rest of the animal's softer, less heavily armored body.

In 2007 fossil claws of a later species of eurypterid called *Jaekelopterus* were found in Germany that are 1 foot 6 inches (46 cm) long. This suggests that the animal itself was more than 8 feet (2.5 m) long, making it the largest known arthropod.

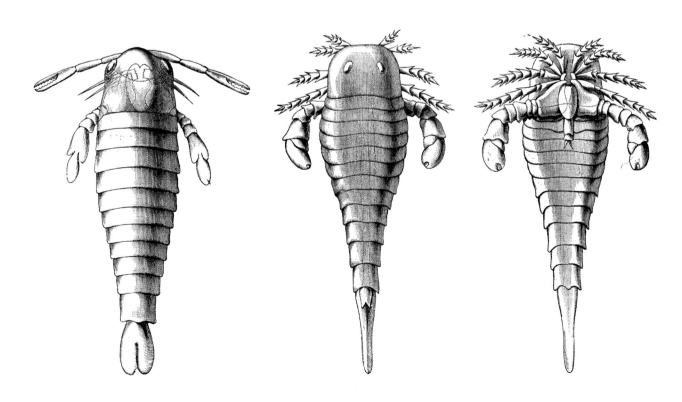

Pneumodesmus

PERIOD: Silurian–Devonian
LOCALITY: Scotland
SIZE: ½ in. (1 cm) long

The strongest candidates for the first truly land-dwelling animals are the ancestors of modern millipedes and centipedes, a group called the myriapods. These were arthropods with long bodies made up of many segments. Millipedes appear in the fossil record before centipedes; they have two pairs of legs on each segment, while centipedes have one.

When the millipede *Pneumodesmus newmani* was found in 2004, it was thought to have lived about 430 million years ago, in the Silurian period. That would make it the oldest known land animal. Later studies, however, suggest it may be 14 million years younger than this. If this is true, it would make *Pneumodesmus* not so special, because other land arthropods are known from the same time.

The species is named after Mike Newman, a bus driver and amateur paleontologist who discovered its fossil at Stonehaven in northeast Scotland. In the Silurian, Scotland formed part of Laurentia, a much larger continent that also included North America. Laurentia lay close to the equator and so would have been warmer than Scotland is today.

We know that *Pneumodesmus* lived on the land, because it had small holes running the length of its body. Myriapods (and also insects) do not breath through mouths or noses but through these holes, which lead to air tubes that reach deep into the body, delivering oxygen to the cells where it is needed. This way of breathing would be useless in the water.

ABOVE: Millipedes such as *Pneumodesmus* were among the first air-breathing animals.

Placoderms and Acanthodians

PLACODERMS
PERIOD: Silurian–Devonian
LOCALITY: Worldwide
SIZE: 10 in.–26 ft.
(25 cm–8 m) long

ACANTHODIANS
PERIOD: Silurian–Permian
LOCALITY: Worldwide
SIZE: 3 in.–3 ft. 3 in.
(7.5 cm–1 m) long

The Devonian period, which lasted from 420 million to 360 million years ago, is sometimes called the age of fishes. Of these fish, the most diverse, common, and spectacular were the placoderms.

Placoderms, which appeared in the earlier Silurian period, were the first vertebrates with mobile jaws bearing teeth, able to grab and bite food. They were also the first with paired fins, which would eventually evolve into arms and legs in land-dwelling vertebrates. Specimens of one 380-million-year-old species, discovered at the Gogo fossil sites in north Western Australia in 2008, contained fossil embryos, making them the first vertebrates known to give birth to live young rather than laying eggs.

But perhaps the most unusual characteristic of placoderms was that their heads and upper bodies were covered in bony plates. This armor, which must have been heavy and cumbersome to carry around, shows that the Devonian ocean was a dangerous place—a fish-eat-fish world, not to mention the threats from invertebrate predators such as nautiloids and sea scorpions.

Most placoderms were predators, either lying in wait for prey close to the seabed or hunting it in the open water. One of the largest, *Dunkleosteus*, grew to be 19 feet 6 inches (6 m) long and had the most powerful bite of any fossil fish, with jaws capable of exerting more than 1,100 pounds (500 kg) of force. Others ate plants, and one of the largest, the 26-foot (8-m) long, 1-ton *Titanichthys*, lacked teeth

LEFT: The placoderm *Dunkleosteus* had the most powerful jaws of any fish.

and may have filtered plankton from the water like some basking, whale, and megamouth sharks do today. Most species, however, were much smaller than these giants.

Placoderms were widely distributed in fresh water as well as the sea. They became extinct at the end of the Devonian period, leaving the seas to two groups of fish: those with bony skeletons, the group to which most modern fish belong and which contain the ancestors of the land vertebrates; and the sharks and rays, whose skeletons are made of flexible cartilage.

Sharks first appeared in the fossil record about 400 million years ago. Along with their relatives, the flat-bodied rays, they rank among some of the most successful and durable predators.

The ancestors of the sharks were a group of extinct fish called the acanthodians, sometimes called the spiny sharks. Like modern sharks, their skeletons were made of cartilage. Because of its softness, cartilage does not fossilize as easily as bone, meaning that the only parts of an acanthodian that were commonly fossilized were the tough spines that held up its fin like the mast of a sailing ship.

Some acanthodians were predators, using their large eyes to find food. Others lacked teeth and were probably filter feeders. Most were relatively small.

Acanthodians appeared in the Silurian period and thrived during the Devonian, living around the globe and colonizing rivers as well as the sea. They became extinct in the Permian period about 250 million years ago.

LEFT: Acanthodians are the ancestors of sharks and rays.

ABOVE: A *Tiktaalik* fossil found in the Canadian Arctic.

OPPOSITE: *Tiktaalik* had strong fins that could have supported its body out of the water.

Tiktaalik

PERIOD: Devonian
LOCALITY: Canada, Greenland
SIZE: 8 ft. (2.5 m) long

*T*iktaalik roseae was a fish that lived 375 million years ago during the Devonian period. However, some aspects of its anatomy look more similar to land-dwelling animals.

It had a flattened head like a crocodile and a mobile neck that meant it could turn its head. It had nostril-like holes on top of its head that could have been used for breathing air. Its fins housed sturdy bones with a joint like a wrist, meaning that they could have propped up the animal's body. These fins may have enabled *Tiktaalik* to push its way along in shallow water, or even to travel short distances out of the water onto shores and riverbanks.

Scientists believe that through these features *Tiktaalik* can provide clues to how vertebrates evolved from fish into land-dwelling animals that walked on legs and breathed air. *Tiktaalik* could not have spent long out of the water, but the rocks in which its fossils are found bear patterns that show they were laid down in a shallow stream, revealing that it lived close to the land. It's impossible to tell whether *Tiktaalik* was a direct ancestor of land vertebrates, such as amphibians and reptiles, but it offers a window into how the journey from water onto land may have taken place.

Tiktaalik was discovered on Ellesmere Island in Arctic Canada. It was big, growing more than 8 feet (up to 2.5 m) long—its name means "large freshwater fish" in the local Inuit language—and it had the sharp teeth of a predator. Like a crocodile, it would have cruised rivers and swamps, using its powerful fins and mobile neck to hunt in water too shallow for other fish, and possibly making forays onto land either to snap up small invertebrates or to escape from predators.

Acanthostega
and Ichthyostega

ACANTHOSTEGA
PERIOD: Devonian
LOCALITY: Greenland
SIZE: 2 ft. (60 cm) long

ICHTHYOSTEGA
PERIOD: Devonian
LOCALITY: Greenland
SIZE: 3 ft. 3 in. (1 m) long

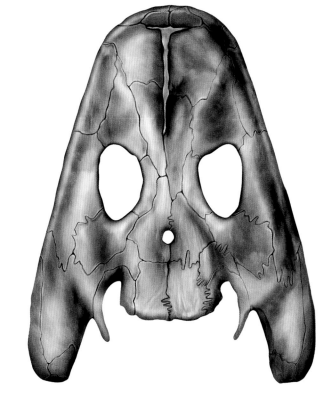

*A*canthostega and *Ichthyostega* are two of the oldest known vertebrates with legs. This makes them vital clues in the mystery of how vertebrates evolved from fish to amphibians. These two animals, however, show that the first vertebrate legs were not the most appropriate for walking. The legs of *Acanthostega gunnari* were like paddles, and it's thought that it would have spent most, if not all, of its life in the water. Judging from its body shape and the fossil water plants in the sites in Greenland, where it has been found, scientists think that *Acanthostega* lived in rivers and shallow swamps, where it used its legs for pushing its way through the vegetation, hunting for small prey animals.

   Acanthostega is regarded as a link between fish species with sturdy, limb-like fins, such as *Tiktaalik*, and the first animals capable of living

62

BELOW: *Acanthostega* had legs but lived in the water.

ABOVE RIGHT: Skull of *Acanthostega*.

OPPOSITE: *Acanthostega* (left) and *Ichthyostega* (center and right) were swamp dwellers.

on land. It had a flat, fishy head, gills for breathing in water, and a large tail fin that would have made it a powerful swimmer. But it also had lungs and could have gulped air above the water. It had webbed feet with fingers and toes, but no wrists or ankles, meaning that its legs would not have been able to support its weight on land. Fossils of *Acanthostega* reach about 2 feet (60 cm) long, although the annual growth rings in the bone structure of the best-preserved fossils hint that they came from young animals that had not yet finished growing.

The discovery of *Acanthostega* changed our views of why vertebrates evolved limbs and how they moved onto land. It suggested that the first vertebrate limbs did not evolve primarily to help animals move and support themselves out of the water. Instead, they were adaptations for life in water that later turned out to be useful for moving around on land.

Ichthyostega was a larger relative of *Acanthostega*, reaching more than 3 feet 3 inches (1 m) long. It would have also spent most of its life in the water—it, too, had a powerful tail and gills. But it also appears to have been better adapted for life on land than *Acanthostega*. Its ribs and limbs, which have seven fingers and toes—compared to eight in *Acanthostega*—are stronger and better able to take its weight. Even so, it was not able to walk as land vertebrates do now. Instead, it probably used its front legs to pull itself slowly across the land, like a seal crossing a beach, with its hind legs providing some extra support.

Both *Acanthostega* and *Ichthyostega* are known from fossils discovered in Greenland, which during the Devonian period was attached to North America and Europe in a landmass known as Laurussia, with a much warmer climate than Greenland has today.

Arthropleura

PERIOD: Carboniferous–Permian
LOCALITY: Europe, North America
SIZE: 6 ft. 6 in. (2 m) long

The Carboniferous period, 340 million to 280 million years ago, was a time of giant bugs. There were dragonflies the size of large birds, cockroaches as big as mice, and scorpions more than 1 foot 7½ inches (50 cm) long. *Arthropleura*—the largest land-living invertebrate that has been found—was the biggest bug of them all.

No complete fossils have been discovered, but from studying fragments and fossil tracks, scientists think that *Arthropleura* grew to be 6 feet 6 inches (2 m) long—longer than most people—and

1 foot 7½ inches (50 cm) wide. It's a relative of modern millipedes, but the largest living millipede is only about 1 foot 3¾ inches (40 cm) long, one-fifth of the size of its ancient relative.

Arthropleura was covered from head to tail in plates made from chitin, a tough substance also found in insect exoskeletons. Based on the depth of the anthropod's tracks, some researchers think the plates must have been thick and heavy; others have suggested its plates were thin and that it relied on its huge size to protect it from predators. In fact, there were no large reptiles, birds, or mammals on

BELOW: *Arthropleura* was the largest land-dwelling invertebrate of all time.

land at this point in Earth's history. Combined with the high level of oxygen in the air, these factors might explain why arthropods were able to grow so large in the Carboniferous period.

The name *Arthropleura* covers a group of half a dozen species of extinct giant millipede. Its fossils are known from the United States, Canada, Great Britain, France, Germany, and Holland. In the Carboniferous period, all these areas were tropical swamps, thickly forested with tree ferns and other early plants. No fossils of its mouth have been found, but scientists believe that, like modern millipedes, it was herbivorous. Fossil dung thought to be from *Arthropleura* contains plant spores, providing some support for this idea.

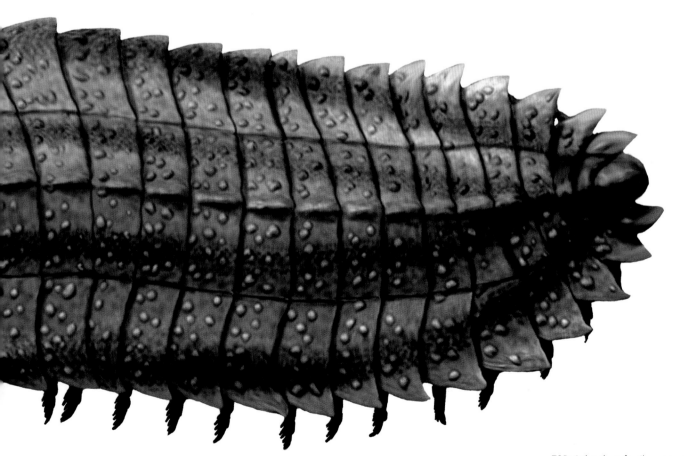

TOP: *Arthropleura* fossil; no complete specimens have been found.

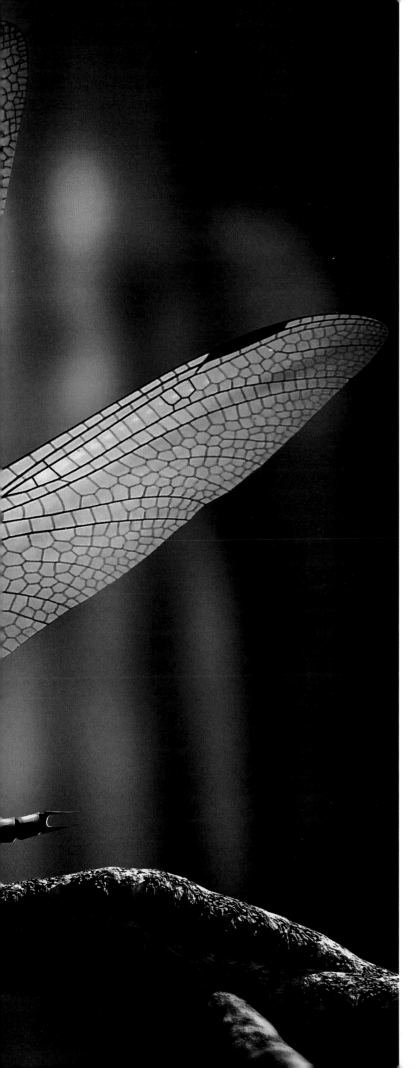

Meganeura

The griffinflies were among the most spectacular insects of the Carboniferous period. *Meganeura* and its relatives had wingspans of up to 2 feet 3½ inches (70 cm), about the same as a pigeon. In comparison, the largest modern dragonflies—the closest living relatives of the griffinflies—have a wingspan of about 7½ inches (19 cm), less than one-third of their ancient relatives.

Like modern dragonflies, *Meganeura* would have been a predator. It flew over rivers, lakes, and other open areas, swooping down on smaller insect prey that it spotted with its excellent compound eyes. It lived alongside, and no doubt preyed upon, a group of large, extinct plant-eating insects called Palaeodictyoptera, which themselves had wingspans of 1 foot 7½ inches (50 cm).

The larvae of both griffinflies and their prey lived in water. Modern dragonfly larvae, which do the same, are also fierce predators, capable of eating small fish. The larvae of *Meganeura* must have grown to about 1 foot (30 cm) long, making them truly fearsome. Fossils of giant dragonflies are known from North America, Europe, and Asia; *Meganeura* itself was found in France and first described in 1885.

The reasons insects and some other invertebrates grew so big during this period of Earth's history are still being debated. The most popular idea is that there was an increased amount of oxygen in the air. Today, air is about 20 percent oxygen, but during the Carboniferous period, it rose to 35 percent—higher than at any time before or since. Oxygen fuels growth, so perhaps insects were able to grow larger as a result.

Higher levels of oxygen were due to the great forests that sprang up in the Carboniferous; huge numbers of trees pumped out oxygen while at the same time removing carbon dioxide from the air. Later, buried in swamps, these plants became fossilized as coal—the carbon that gives the period its name. Now, as we burn these deposits for energy, we are releasing their carbon to the atmosphere and raising the level of carbon dioxide.

ONTO LAND

67

LEFT: The griffinfly *Meganeura* was the size of a bird.

Hylonomus

PERIOD: Carboniferous
LOCALITY: Canada
SIZE: 10 in. (25 cm) long

*H*ylonomus lyelli is the oldest known animal widely agreed to be a reptile. There are other candidates from earlier in life's history, but they can't definitively be identified as reptiles. *Hylonomus* looked much like a lizard, although it belongs to an extinct group that is not related to any living species. It probably also lived much like a lizard, scuttling through the forest and hunting for insects and millipedes. It was about 10 inches (25 cm) long, including its tail.

The oldest fossil skeletons of *Hylonomus* are about 312 million years old, from toward the end of the Carboniferous period. Fossil footprints a few million years older that are thought to have been made by the same animal have also been found.

The first fossils of *Hylonomus* were discovered more than 150 years ago on the Canadian island of Nova Scotia, which lay in the tropics during the Carboniferous period. The fossils were found inside another fossil of a hollow tree stump—the name *Hylonomus* means "forest dweller." It is thought that the stump was left behind when the rest of the tree rotted away, creating a space that was either a home for small animals or a trap that they fell into and could not climb out of. These trees grew far away from the water, indicating that *Hylonomus* had evolved to spend its life on land. Reptiles are well adapted to dry places, thanks to scaly skins that prevent their bodies from losing water. Their eggs also have leathery shells that do not dry out.

Hylonomus is the oldest known of several similar species found in the same Canadian rocks. These early reptiles would become the dominant land vertebrates for more than 200 million years.

OPPOSITE: *Hylonomus* lived in forests and was discovered in a fossilized tree stump.

ABOVE: Fossilized upper jaw and teeth of *Hylonomus*.

Eryops

PERIOD: Permian
LOCALITY: North America
SIZE: 6 ft. 6 in. (2 m) long

*E*ryops megacephalus was one of the largest members of a highly successful group of amphibians called the temnospondyls, which lived on every continent. They first appeared in the fossil record in the Carboniferous period and survived for more than 200 million years, well into the age of the dinosaurs.

Nearly 300 species are known, making them the most diverse group of early land vertebrates. They shared a similar lizard-like body shape but ranged in size from an inch or two (a few cm) to a massive 30 feet (9 m) long—the length of a bus. Scientific opinion is divided on how they are related to modern amphibians such as frogs and salamanders. Many scientists believe the temnospondyls are direct ancestors, while others contend they are a related group that became extinct.

Eryops, which lived in the Permian period, 295 million years ago, wasn't as big as the largest of its kind, but it was far bigger than any modern amphibian, extending up to 6 feet 6 inches (2 m) long. Like modern amphibians, *Eryops* spent its early life in fresh water breathing through gills before developing the adult ability to survive on land. Unlike frogs and toads, however, which grow from tadpole to adult in a single year, *Eryops* probably spent several years in the water before it developed sufficiently to survive on land.

With its powerful legs, *Eryops* was well adapted for life on land. Traces of its fossilized skin have been found, which show that it was scaly and armored. No living amphibian has this feature, but several contemporaries of *Eryops* did. As an adult, *Eryops* would have been an efficient walker but not a fast runner. It probably fed in the water, where it would have been more agile, hunting animals in ponds and rivers. Its huge mouth was filled with sharp, backward-pointing teeth, which would have made them good for gripping slippery prey. Fossils of large early amphibians have been found with fish in their stomachs.

LEFT: As an amphibian, *Eryops* needed to return to the water to breed.

BELOW: *Eryops* skeleton, showing the animal's sturdy legs and mouth full of sharp teeth.

Dimetrodon and Procynosuchus

DIMETRODON
PERIOD: Permian
LOCALITY: North America, Europe
SIZE: 13 ft. (4 m) long

PROCYNOSUCHUS
PERIOD: Permian
LOCALITY: Europe, Africa
SIZE: 2 ft. (60 cm) long

These animals resembled dinosaurs, but both were more closely related to mammals. They belong to a group called the synapsids. Before the dinosaurs, this was the most widespread, diverse, and dominant group of land vertebrates for tens of millions of years.

Dimetrodon has been called the oldest known, fully land-living apex predator; it was the top hunter of its time, occupying the pinnacle of the food chain with no predators of its own. The name *Dimetrodon* is used to describe a group of about a dozen species, ranging in size from 2 feet (60 cm) to nearly 16 feet 6 inches (5 m)

long, that lived in the early Permian period, between about 295 million and 270 million years ago. The larger species were ferocious, intimidating animals, weighing up to 600 pounds (300 kg), which is more than a fully grown grizzly bear.

Fossils of *Dimetrodon* have been found in Texas and Oklahoma, as well as in Germany, with tracks discovered in New Mexico and in Nova Scotia, Canada. During the Permian, North America and Europe, along with all of Earth's other landmasses, were fused into a single supercontinent called Pangaea. All species were predators, with teeth specialized for stabbing and cutting. The largest species

had teeth with jagged, serrated edges like steak knives, which would have been good for hunting tough-skinned prey.

For a long time, scientists have been puzzled about why *Dimetrodon* had such a large sail on its back. It was once thought that the sail, which was held up by bony spines growing out of the animal's backbone, was used to help the animal absorb the sun's warmth in cold weather and radiate heat away when it got too hot. But scientists now believe that the sail would not have been good at heat regulation and think it was probably an ornament for intimidating rivals or impressing potential mates, like a peacock's tail.

Procynosuchus was another synapsid, although a much smaller one than most species of *Dimetrodon*, being 2 feet (60 cm) long at its largest. It was one of the oldest known members of a group called the cynodonts, ancestors of modern mammals. Cynodonts have been key to our understanding of how later mammals, including humans, evolved.

Procynosuchus lived later than *Dimetrodon*, toward the end of the Permian period, 250 million years ago. Its fossils have been found in Germany and the African countries of Zambia and South Africa, showing that it roamed widely across Pangaea.

It had a long, powerful tail, wide feet, and powerful back legs. These may have been adaptations for swimming, and it may have spent a lot of its time in the water, like a modern otter. Later cynodonts may have been warm-blooded, although there is no evidence that they had fur.

Otters dig burrows, and at least some cynodonts of this time, such as *Thrinaxodon*, were also burrowers. A fossil in a burrow stands out, because the remains of a hole that has been filled with sediment—in a flood, for example—look different from the surrounding rock. Burrowing may have helped the cynodonts survive the environmental changes at the end of the Permian that gradually wiped out so much of the rest of animal life.

OPPOSITE: *Dimetrodon* was a synapsid, the dominant group of land vertebrates for tens of millions of years.

ABOVE: Cynodonts such as *Procynosuchus* are the ancestors of mammals.

Dimetrodon was the world's largest land
predator up to that point in time.

3

THE AGE OF
DINOSAURS

OPPOSITE: The armored dinosaur *Stegosaurus* lived in the
Jurassic period, about 150 million years ago.

PERIOD

TRIASSIC (251–199 million years ago)
JURASSIC (199–145 million years ago)
CRETACEOUS (145–66 million years ago)

Ever since they were first discovered, dinosaurs have held human imagination in a grip as strong as the jaws of a *Tyrannosaurus rex*. If anything, our fascination has grown as we have learned that they were not lumbering giants marked for extinction, but fast, dynamic animals with sophisticated behaviors and complex social lives.

The first dinosaurs appeared late in the Triassic period, about 220 million years ago. The first mammals evolved around the same time, as did the flying pterosaurs, and marine reptiles such as plesiosaurs and ichthyosaurs.

During the Triassic, the single landmass Pangaea separated into Gondwana in the south and Laurasia in the north. Where North America separated from Africa, the spreading continents created another enormous burst of volcanic eruptions and another period of rapid climate change.

These eruptions are the prime suspect for the mass extinctions that marked the end of the Triassic. More than three-quarters of species became extinct. Dinosaurs escaped relatively lightly, and the disappearance of so many other species cleared the way for them to become the dominant large land animals of the Jurassic and Cretaceous periods.

During the Jurassic, the climate became warmer and wetter. Regions that had been deserts in the Triassic became forests filled with conifers. Tropical plants lived as far north as Canada.

LEFT: Nineteenth-century interpretations of *Iguanodon* (left and center) and *Hylaeosaurus*.

OPPOSITE: "Sue," one of the most complete skeletons of *Tyrannosaurus rex*.

In the Cretaceous period, the continents we recognize today moved toward their current positions. Each developed its own distinct dinosaur species, recorded in spectacular fossil deposits found in Montana and Utah, as well as China's Gobi Desert. The biggest dinosaurs of all, the sauropods, lived in South America.

The world we live in now was shaped by two phenomena that occurred during the Cretaceous. One was creative: the origin and rapid evolution of flowering plants and the insects they rely on for pollination. The other was destructive: the asteroid that collided with Earth 66 million years ago.

In 1980 the geologist Walter Alvarez and his father Luis showed that the rocks laid down at the end of the Cretaceous contained a thin layer of iridium. This element is rare on Earth but is much more common in rocks from space.

Rock layers from the end of the Cretaceous are also rich in what is called shocked quartz, with crystals that bear the imprint of extreme pressure. These two pieces of evidence along with the discovery off Mexico's Yucatán Peninsula of the remains of a crater 93 miles (150 km) across and 12½ miles (20 km) deep, made a compelling case for a destructive asteroid impact.

The asteroid was at least 6¼ miles (10 km) across and was traveling at more than 44,000 miles per hour (70,000 km/h) when it hit with the force of a billion nuclear bombs. The impact sent tsunamis rushing around the planet and set forests on fire 1,000 miles (1,600 km) away. Ash and dust plunged Earth into darkness for months.

Three-quarters of all species were wiped out. Whether this impact was the true killer blow, or whether environmental changes had already put these species on the road to extinction, is still debated. What is certain is that life's slate was wiped almost completely clean once again.

THE MOVEMENT OF THE CONTINENTS IN THE MESOZOIC ERA

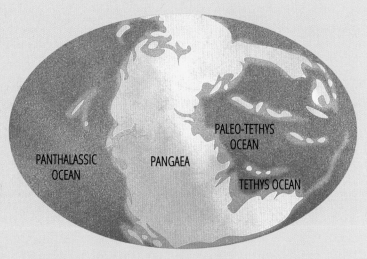

EARLY TRIASSIC

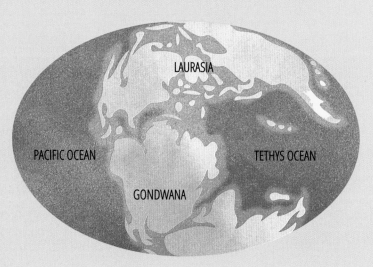

LATE JURASSIC

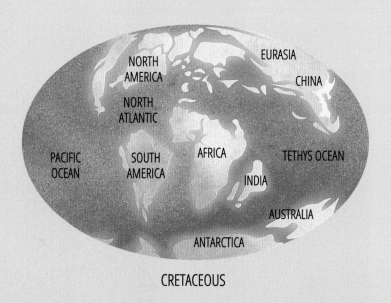

CRETACEOUS

OPPOSITE: Ammonite mollusks that lived in the seas for 350 million years disappeared at the end of the Cretaceous.

TOP: Ginkgo trees have changed little since this fossil was formed 160 million years ago.

RIGHT: *Leefructus* from China is one of the earliest flowering plants.

Lystrosaurus

PERIOD: Triassic
DISTRIBUTION: Asia, Africa, Antarctica
SIZE: 3 ft. 3 in. (1 m) long

T he mass extinction at the end of the Permian period wiped out so many animals that the survivors found themselves in a far less crowded and competitive world. *Lystrosaurus* was one of the fortunate ones, and it made the most of its luck. In the early Triassic period, from about 250 million years ago, it was the most common land vertebrate.

No animal before or since has dominated the land to such as extent. For an extended time, nineteen out of every twenty land vertebrates were *Lystrosaurus*. It wouldn't be too much of an exaggeration to say that these animals ruled Earth for millions of years.

Lystrosaurus was a synapsid, which includes *Dimetrodon* and the cynodonts that had thrived in the Permian. Like them, it was a reptile with some mammalian characteristics—it may have had hair and been warm-blooded. More than twenty species of *Lystrosaurus*

are known. Most were about 3 feet 3 inches (1 m) long and had a stocky build, about the size and shape of a pig. All had a horny beak like a turtle, two tusks, and no teeth.

Lystrosaurus was a herbivore. Scientists believe that it used its tusks for digging, because fossils have been found in burrows. The ability to burrow may have been one reason it survived changes in temperature and other environmental shifts that killed off so many other species. Tusks may also have been used for fighting over mates and warding off predators. These animals may have spent much of their time in the water, swimming in pools and rivers like small hippopotamuses.

Its fossils have been found in bone beds in what is now Antarctica, India, China, Mongolia, the Moscow Basin of Russia, and the Balfour and Katburg formations of South Africa. At the time, all these were joined into a single supercontinent.

82

BELOW: A fossil skull of *Lystrosaurus* from South Africa.

OPPOSITE: *Lystrosaurus* was the most common land vertebrate in the Triassic period.

Eoraptor

*E*oraptor lunensis was one of the first dinosaurs. Its name means "dawn thief"—"dawn" because it is one of the earliest known of its kind and "thief" because its anatomy suggests a skillful hunter. It was able to run fast, and it had long claws on three of its five fingers. Even so, it was not as specialized for meat eating as some later dinosaurs. It had sharp, pointed teeth in its upper jaw like a meat eater, and smaller, leaf-shaped teeth in its lower jaw like a plant eater, meaning it probably ate a mixture of foods.

Eoraptor lived 228 million years ago, in the middle of the Triassic period, when dinosaurs were relatively rare and outnumbered by other types of large reptiles. It was about 3 feet 3 inches (1 m) long and weighed about 22 pounds (10 kg). It had long back legs and short arms, suggesting that it stood upright and ran on its back legs like a bird. Most dinosaur species of the time did the same.

Named in 1993, *Eoraptor* was discovered in the fossil remains of a forest in northwest Argentina. Dinosaurs did not become the dominant large animals until late in the Triassic period, following a wave of extinctions among other large reptiles.

Partly because it was not specialized for either plant or meat eating, scientists have been puzzled about where *Eoraptor* fits into the dinosaur lineage. Some believe it is an early member of the theropods, the group of meat eaters that includes *Tyrannosaurus rex* and *Velociraptor*. Others believe it belongs with the sauropods, the herbivorous group that included giants such as *Diplodocus*.

TOP: Skull of *Eoraptor*, showing the sharp teeth in its upper jaw.

ABOVE: *Eoraptor*, one of the earliest dinosaurs, was discovered in Argentina.

Megazostrodon

Megazostrodon rudnerae, one of the earliest known mammals, would have fit within the palm of your hand. It was only 4 inches (10 cm) from head to tail and weighed about an ounce (20–30 g). That's about the size of a modern shrew. It also had a pointy snout and teeth similar to a shrew, and so, like them, it probably ate small insects. It lived 200 million years ago in what is now southern Africa.

One thing that sets mammals such as *Megazostrodon* apart from reptiles is that they have more specialized teeth, with some shaped for cutting, some for tearing, and others for crushing food. This diversity enables mammals to chew their food more thoroughly and so extract more nutrients from it, helping to support an active lifestyle.

Mammals require more calories than reptiles because they are warm-blooded and need to maintain a constant body temperature. This is a feature that, along with fur, mammals inherited from their ancestors such as the cynodonts. A warm-blooded animal can remain active at cooler temperatures that would make a cold-blooded reptile—which relies on its outside environment to provide body heat—sluggish.

Many mammals seem to have taken advantage of this ability to remain active in cool conditions by becoming nocturnal. Scans of the inside of a *Megazostrodon* skull reveal that *Megazostrodon* had well-developed brain areas for hearing and smell—senses that are especially useful in the dark. Evolving to be active during the night would have helped mammals to avoid dinosaurs and other reptiles that hunted in the daytime.

Some features of *Megazostrodon*, however, were not like today's mammals. For example, it held its legs at the side of its body like a lizard rather than underneath it as modern mammals do. It therefore would not have been as fast or nimble as a shrew.

ABOVE: The shrewlike *Megazostrodon* was one of the earliest mammals.

PERIOD: Triassic
LOCALITY: Europe, Asia, Greenland
SIZE: 3 ft. 3 in. (1 m) long

Proganochelys

Turtles and tortoises are an old group that split from the rest of the reptiles during the Permian period, about 260 million years ago. The earliest species looked more like lizards than tortoises. They did not have shells and had mouths full of teeth, unlike modern tortoises and turtles, which have beaks.

These ancient animals did, however, have wide rib cages, which over tens of millions of years of evolution developed into an armored shell protecting the body. We can see the completion of that process in *Proganochelys quenstedti*—probably the oldest known species that a time traveler would have no trouble recognizing as a tortoise.

Proganochelys had a fully developed shell, covering both its back and its belly, as well as a beak, suggesting that, like its modern relatives, it ate plants. However, there were some differences between *Proganochelys* and modern tortoises; for example, it could not pull its head back into its shell. It also had a spiny, club-like tail that no modern tortoise possesses.

Proganochelys lived in the late Triassic, 210 million years ago. Its fossils were first found in Germany, which at that time formed part of the giant northern continent of Laurasia. Related species have also been found in Thailand and Greenland, which would have been part of the same landmass.

The animal was about 3 feet 3 inches (1 m) long. This is large by the standards of modern land-dwelling tortoises, although it is not large for a sea turtle. A 2018 study that used scans of the animal's skull to work out the shape of its brain showed that *Proganochelys* probably had a good sense of smell but poor sight and hearing.

There is less certainty over how *Proganochelys* lived. Some paleontologists have suggested that it was a good swimmer, spending much of its time in the water; others believe it stayed on land and may have been a burrower. While its shell does bear similarities to those of aquatic species, its limbs appear better suited to walking than swimming. One possibility is that *Proganochelys* was not highly adapted for life on either land or water, and that adaptations for more specialized ways of living evolved only in later species.

LEFT: *Proganochelys* was the oldest known tortoise with a full shell.

87

Scelidosaurus

PERIOD: Jurassic
LOCALITY: Europe
SIZE: 13 ft. (4 m) long

As the meat-eating dinosaurs got larger—and, no doubt, smarter—and their claws and teeth became sharper, different groups of plant-eating dinosaurs evolved new ways to protect themselves. Some species became so big they were practically invulnerable; some found safety in numbers by living in herds; others developed armor and weaponry.

Scelidosaurus harrisonii is an example of the third strategy. It is one of the oldest members of a group of armored herbivorous dinosaurs called the thyreophorans, dating from early in the Jurassic period, about 195 million years ago. This is around the time when dinosaurs had started to become the dominant land vertebrates. The first fossil was discovered in England, which was then part of a group of tropical islands.

Later thyreophorans include the stegosaurs, which had bony plates down their backs, and *Ankylosaurus*, which had heavy armor and a club at the end of its tail. *Scelidosaurus* was less heavily armored than some of these later species, but it was still well defended, covered from head to tail in bony, spiked plates. It was also more than 13 feet (4 m) long and weighed about 660 pounds

(300 kg). It probably walked mostly on four legs; however, based on fossil dinosaur tracks, some scientists have suggested that it could also have stood and walked on its hind legs.

Scelidosaurus occupies a special place in the study of dinosaurs. The British paleontologist David Norman called it "the first ever, more or less complete dinosaur discovered." Its bones were found in 1858, and the species was described and named by Richard Owen, the founder of London's Natural History Museum and the man who invented the word "dinosaur," meaning "terrible reptile." The animal's remains were found in the famous fossil-bearing cliffs of Dorset, on England's south coast, a region now known as the Jurassic Coast. It's the most complete dinosaur skeleton that has been found in Great Britain.

BELOW: *Scelidosaurus* was covered with bony, spiked plates.

OPPOSITE ABOVE: *Scelidosaurus* is the most complete dinosaur found in Great Britain.

OPPOSITE BELOW: A nineteenth-century interpretation of *Scelidosaurus*.

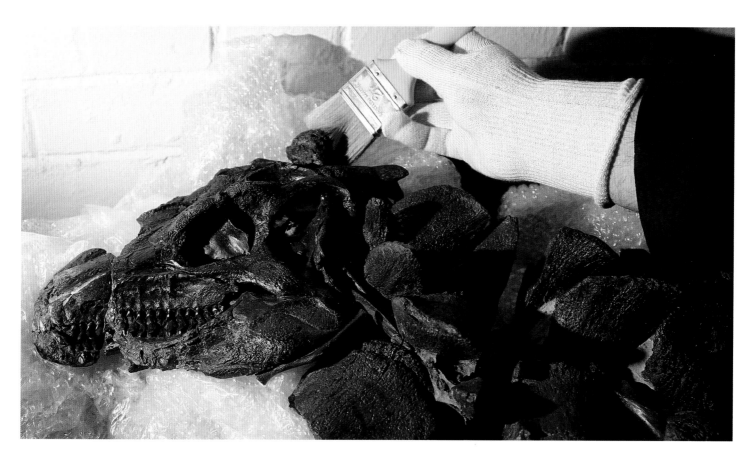

Ophthalmosaurus and Liopleurodon

OPHTHALMOSAURUS
PERIOD: Jurassic
LOCALITY: Europe, North America
SIZE: 13 ft. (4 m) long

LIOPLEURODON
PERIOD: Jurassic
LOCALITY: Europe
SIZE: 23 ft. (7 m) long

Today the only reptiles truly at home in the sea are turtles and the saltwater crocodile—and even they need to leave the water to lay their eggs on land. However, for 110 million years, from the Triassic to the end of the Cretaceous, reptiles were among the biggest animals in the seas. Two of the most successful types were the ichthyosaurs such as *Ophthalmosaurus* and the plesiosaurs such as *Liopleurodon*.

Like such marine mammals as dolphins and seals, the ancient marine reptiles are descended from land-living ancestors, and both ichthyosaurs and plesiosaurs reflected these origins in having four flippers.

Ophthalmosaurus, which lived in the middle of the Jurassic period, was given its name for its enormous eyes, which could be more than 8 inches (20 cm) in diameter—the largest of any vertebrate. These would have been excellent for seeing in low light, possibly when the animal dived in pursuit of fish and squid. The remains of both food sources have been found in the stomachs of fossil ichthyosaurs. *Ophthalmosaurus* measured about 13 feet (4 m) from snout to tail, similar to a great white shark. Other species of ichthyosaurs could reach more than 65 feet (20 m) long.

While ichthyosaurs had bodies that resembled a dolphin's and swam by beating their tails from side to side like fish, the plesiosaurs are harder to compare with any living animal. For example, they were the only aquatic animals that swam by paddling with all four flippers at the same time. Other flipper-powered swimmers, such as penguins and sea turtles, use only their front limbs, letting their back legs trail behind them. Experiments with robots show that four-flippered swimming is better for short, fast bursts than sustained cruising, so plesiosaurs may have lain in wait and pounced on their prey instead of chasing it down.

Some plesiosaurs had long necks. *Liopleurodon ferox* wasn't one of them; instead it had a short neck and a massive skull that could be more than 3 feet 3 inches (1 m) long. Armed with 4-inch (10-cm) teeth and capable of biting with incredible force, it would have been able to kill whatever it grabbed between its jaws. Plesiosaurs with this body shape are called pliosaurs, the largest of which could reach more than 33 feet (10 m) long. *Liopleurodon* was smaller than this, at about 23 feet (7 m) long.

Unlike most modern, land-living reptiles, ichthyosaurs and plesiosaurs gave birth to live young. Dozens of fossil females containing embryos have been found, some even preserved in the act of giving birth. It's thought that they were warm-blooded, and some exceptionally well-preserved ichthyosaur fossils even show a layer of blubber, the fatty tissue that dolphins, whales, and seals use to maintain body heat in the sea.

Ophthalmosaurus icenicus was identified from fossils found in Cambridgeshire in England, while *Liopleurodon* was first found near Boulogne in northern France. It's possible that the two species shared the Tethys Ocean that covered much of Europe at that time. Ichthyosaurs, plesiosaurs, and many other kinds of marine reptiles became extinct in the Cretaceous period. Ichthyosaurs vanish from the fossil record about 90 million years ago. One theory is that they could not evolve quickly enough to adapt to a period of rapid global warming. Plesiosaurs seem to have survived longer, disappearing at the end of the Cretaceous, 65 million years ago, in the same mass extinction that killed the dinosaurs.

OPPOSITE: The marine reptile *Ophthalmosaurus* had the largest eyes of any vertebrate.

FOLLOWING PAGES: With massive jaws and teeth like knives, *Liopleurodon* was a ferocious predator.

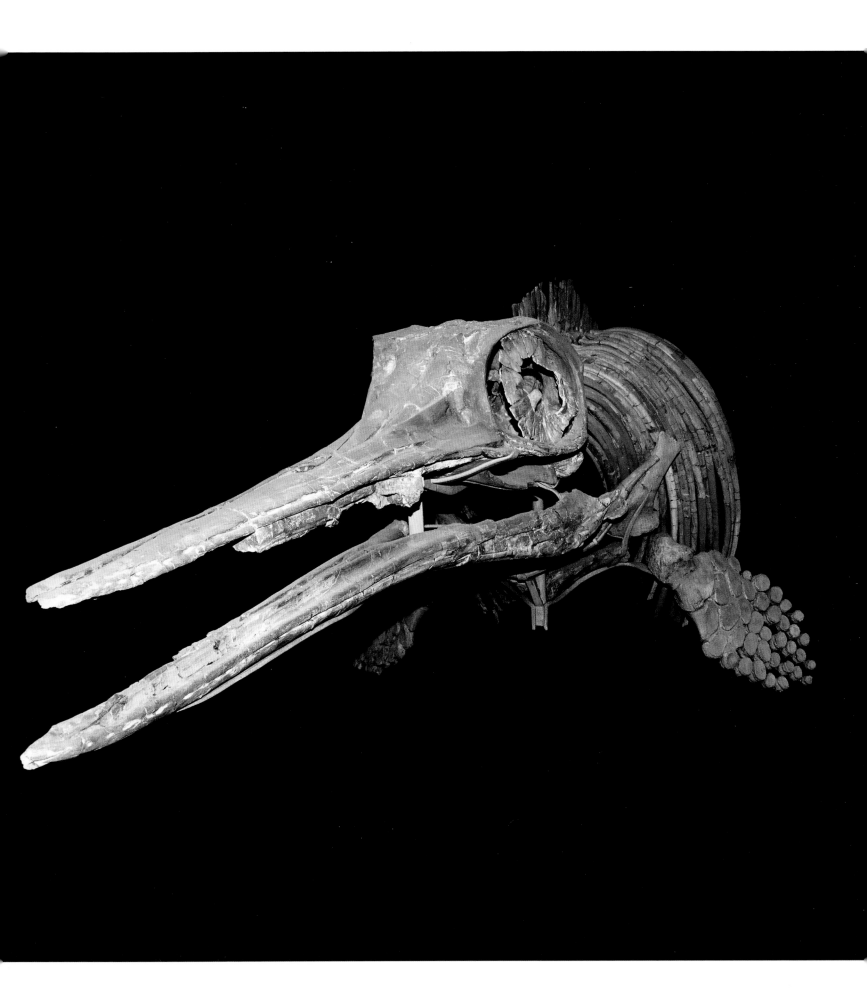

Archaeopteryx

PERIOD: Jurassic
LOCALITY: Europe
SIZE: 1 ft. 7½ in. (50 cm) long

*A*rchaeopteryx lithographica was discovered in 1861. Two years previously, Charles Darwin had set out his theory of evolution in *On the Origin of Species*. If, as Darwin suggested, animals changed over time, evolving from one form into another, there should be missing links, animals that represented a point on that journey and that combined features from creatures at either end of the line. *Archaeopteryx* fitted that bill remarkably well, making it a crucial piece of evidence for the truth of evolution. It was a dinosaur with birdlike features—wings covered in feathers that formed an airfoil and a large fanlike tail. Yet, like a reptile, it also had teeth in its beak, claws on its wings, and a bony tail.

Archaeopteryx lived about 150 million years ago. The first fossil was discovered in the Solnhofen Limestone Formation in Bavaria, Germany, one of the rare sites where soft and delicate features—in this case feathers—are preserved. Since then, ten more have been found, most of them in the same area. *Archaeopteryx* was about the size of a large crow, 1 foot 7½ inches (50 cm) long and weighing up to 2 pounds 4 ounces (1 kg). It would have been a hunter, probably catching insects along with small reptiles and mammals. Its long tail would have made it look like an American scrub jay or a European magpie. Pigments called melanosomes detected in its feathers suggest that it was at least partly black, although the exact colors and patterns of its plumage cannot be determined.

In fact, despite 150 years of study, there is still a great deal we don't know about *Archaeopteryx*. Scientists disagree, for example, about whether it could truly fly or only glide and, if it did fly, whether it became airborne by launching itself from a tree or running along the ground and jumping up. If it could fly, it probably moved its wings differently than modern birds and would not have been able to cover long distances or reach high speeds.

More recent discoveries of other feathered dinosaurs and early birds have led researchers to think that today's birds are not descended directly from *Archaeopteryx*. However, it always will occupy a special place in our understanding of evolution and ancient life.

OPPOSITE: Fossils of *Archaeopteryx* were found in Germany in 1861.

ABOVE: *Archaeopteryx* had a mixture of birdlike and reptilian features.

Sordes and Quetzalcoatlus

SORDES
PERIOD: Jurassic
LOCALITY: Asia
SIZE: 1 ft. (30 cm) long,
wingspan 23½ inches (60 cm)

QUETZALCOATLUS
PERIOD: Cretaceous
LOCALITY: North America
SIZE: 30 ft. (9 m) long,
wingspan 33 ft. (10 m)

Birdlike dinosaurs weren't the first vertebrates to take to the sky. That honor goes to the pterosaurs, a group of reptiles that first appeared in the late Triassic period, nearly 230 million years ago, and disappeared 65 million years ago, another victim of the mass extinction at the end of the Cretaceous.

Pterosaurs lived worldwide—their fossils have been found from Greenland to Antarctica, and from Japan to Great Britain. And they evolved to thrive in every environment, from skimming or diving into the sea for fish to plucking fruit and insects from the trees to hunting animals on the ground. The smallest species had a wingspan of about 10 inches (25 cm), slightly bigger than a European robin. At their greatest size, they were the largest flying creatures Earth has ever seen.

Sordes pilosus was on the small side, with a wingspan of about 23½ inches (60 cm). It lived toward the end of the Jurassic period, about 155 million years ago, and its fossils were discovered in the remains of an ancient lake in Kazakhstan.

Its body shape, with a long tail, is similar to that of many early pterosaurs. It had a relatively large skull, with fang-like teeth at the front of its mouth and crushing teeth in the back. These would have been good for grabbing prey, such as insects, amphibians, and small lizards, and then breaking them up for swallowing.

Discovered in 1971, *Sordes* was the first pterosaur fossil to provide evidence that these animals had hair, with short fuzz on their bodies and longer hair on the wings. Its name means "hairy filth" and was inspired by the evil spirits of Kazakh folklore. Its layer of insulation

LEFT: *Sordes* (right and top left) was the first pterosaur shown to have a hairy body in the fossil record.

OPPOSITE: The giant pterosaur *Quetzalcoatlus* had a bony skull crest.

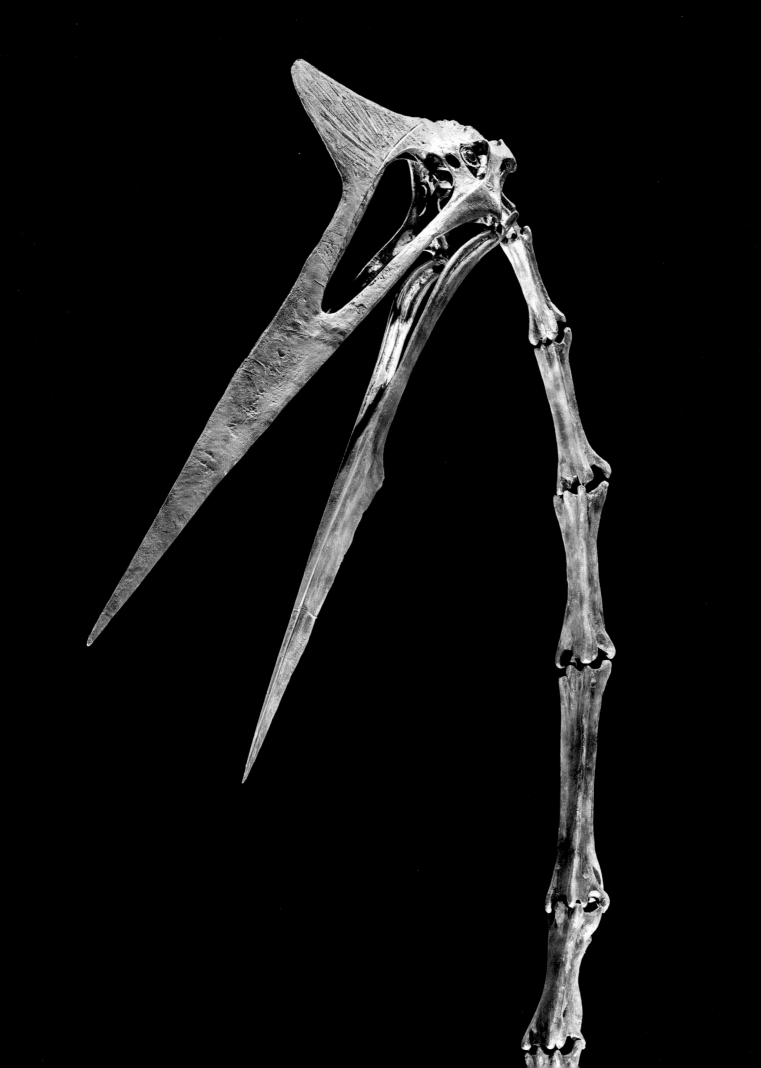

would have helped *Sordes* maintain a constant body temperature, and therefore higher levels of activity, instead of simply letting its temperature fluctuate with the surrounding environment. In other words, it was warm-blooded, something that scientists believe would have been necessary to supply the energy needed to fly.

Quetzalcoatlus northropi lived later than *Sordes*, dating from the end of the Cretaceous period, about 70 million years ago. And it was much bigger—possibly the biggest pterosaur of all. It had a wingspan of 33 to 36 feet (10–11 m), similar to a small aircraft; it would have stood 10 feet (3 m) tall on the ground and weighed 440 pounds (200 kg) or more. Like many pterosaurs, it had a crest on its skull; some species had crests that grew into weird and wonderful shapes, looking like sails sprouting from the top of the animal's head. These may have been ornaments that attracted mates—in some species, males' crests seem to have been larger than females'.

Named after Quetzlcoatl, the feathered serpent god of the Aztecs, and the US aircraft maker Northrop, *Quetzalcoatlus northropi* lived in what is now North America; its fossils were first discovered at Big Bend National Park in Texas. It may have fed on the ground, walking on all fours to hunt and bending its long neck to snap up prey in its toothless beak like a gargantuan stork as tall as a giraffe.

How—and if—*Quetzalcoatlus* flew is still debated. Some scientists have suggested it was too big to get off the ground; others believe it was capable of soaring long distances on its vast wings. Large pterosaurs such as *Quetzalcoatlus* evolved hollow wing bones, helping them keep their weight down and making it easier to remain airborne. Birdlike dinosaurs evolved hollow bones separately. Like flight itself, this is an example of convergent evolution, where the same trait or ability evolves independently in different groups of species.

LEFT: *Quetzalcoatlus* probably hunted on the ground, walking on all fours.

PERIOD: Jurassic–Cretaceous
LOCALITY: Worldwide
SIZE: 33 ft. (10 m) long

Iguanodon

Iguanodon belonged to one of the largest and most successful groups of plant-eating dinosaurs. It was part of a lineage that began as small, swift-running animals and gradually evolved into much larger species such as the duck-billed hadrosaurs.

Iguanodon bernissartensis lived in the late Jurassic and Cretaceous periods, about 160 million to 100 million years ago. Its fossils have been found across the world in North America, Europe, Asia, Africa, and Australia. It is named after the shape of its teeth, which resemble those of a modern iguana lizard. They were specialized for chewing tough plant material and would have fallen out and been replaced when they wore down.

Iguanodon weighed about 3 tons and measured 33 feet (10 m) from head to tail. It would have held its body horizontally, with its tail extended behind it for balance, and been able to shift between walking on all fours and standing upright. It probably spent most of its time on four legs, grazing and browsing, but scientists believe it was fastest when traveling on its hind legs, with an estimated top speed of 15 miles per hour (24km/h).

One of *Iguanodon*'s most distinctive features was its long thumb spike. This may have been used as a weapon for fighting predators or other members of its own species, as a tool for feeding by stripping

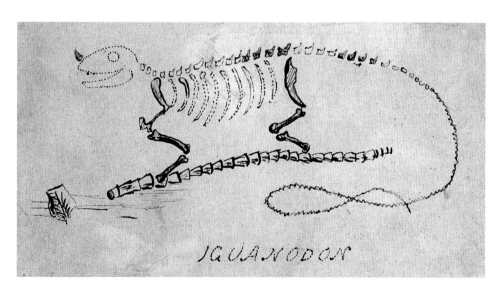

ABOVE: An *Iguanodon* footprint at Compton Bay, Isle of Wight, England.

LEFT: A sketch of *Iguanodon* by the Victorian paleontologist Gideon Mantell.

leaves or cracking seeds, or possibly both. The three middle fingers on its front legs were sturdy and hooflike and could have supported the animal's weight when it walked on all fours. Its little finger was long and flexible, enabling it to hold and manipulate objects.

In 1822 *Iguanodon* was the second dinosaur to be discovered and was found in the southern English county of Sussex. Contemporary accounts suggested that its teeth were noticed by Mary Ann Mantell, glinting in the rock at the side of the road. She was traveling with her husband, Gideon, a physician and amateur paleontologist, who presented the teeth to London's Royal Society. Since then, scientists have changed many of their theories about *Iguanadon*. Its thumb spike, for example, was first thought to be on its nose like a rhinoceros horn.

BELOW: *Iguanodon* hand, showing the spiked thumb and sturdy fingers.

BOTTOM: Fossil skull of *Iguanodon*, showing the back teeth used to grind plants.

Repenomamus

When mammals had to share the world with dinosaurs, they stayed relatively small. With its long, stocky body and short legs, *Repenomamus* would have looked somewhat like a badger. Two closely related species are known— the largest, *Repenomamus giganticus*, measured more than 3 feet 3 inches (1 m) long and would have weighed about 26 pounds 8 ounces (12 kg).

The teeth of *Repenomamus* show that it was a carnivore and probably a predator. One specimen discovered in Liaoning in northeast China was found with the bones of a baby dinosaur called *Psittacosaurus* in its stomach. The baby could have been snatched from an unattended nest, but it's also possible that *Repenomamus* was a scavenger, feeding on the bodies of animals that were already dead. As well as young dinosaurs, its diet may also have included worms and insects.

Repenomamus lived early in the Cretaceous period, 125 million years ago. Its skeleton shows that it either laid eggs, like a few modern mammals, such as the duck-billed platypus, or gave birth to small, undeveloped young like modern marsupials.

It belonged to a large group of extinct carnivorous mammals not closely related to any living species. Other members of the group seem to have been specialized for swimming, while others appear to have had flaps of skin between their legs that they used for gliding like modern flying squirrels. While mammals of this time may have lived in the shadow of the dinosaurs, they were already a diverse group with species adapted to many different habitats and ways of life.

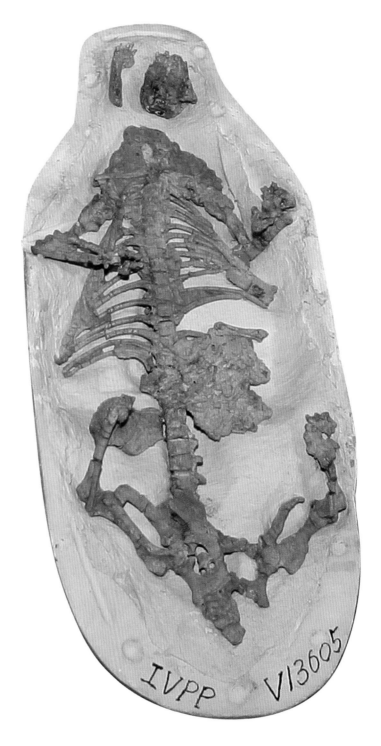

RIGHT: This *Repenomamus* fossil from Lianoning, China, has the remains of a baby dinosaur in its stomach.

SINOSAUROPTERYX
PERIOD: Cretaceous
LOCALITY: Asia
SIZE: 3 ft. 3 in. (1 m) long

ANCHIORNIS
PERIOD: Jurassic
LOCALITY: Asia
SIZE: 1 ft. 7½ in. (50 cm) long

Sinosauropteryx and Anchiornis

RIGHT: *Anchiornis* may have been able to glide on its feathered arms.

Not all the dinosaurs are extinct. There's probably one perching in a tree, pecking at the ground, or flying through the air not far from where you are right now. Today's birds are descended from a group of two-legged predatory dinosaurs called the theropods, which included such well-known species as *Tyrannosaurus rex*.

A crucial step on the journey from dinosaur to bird was the evolution of feathers. Important discoveries that showed birds were descended from dinosaurs (and not some other type of reptile) came in the mid-1990s, when paleontologists working in Liaoning Province in northeast China began to uncover amazingly well-preserved fossils of animals that were clearly feathered dinosaurs. *Sinosauropteryx prima*—the name means "first Chinese dragon bird"—was the first of these to be found, by a farmer and part-time fossil hunter in 1996.

Sinosauropteryx was small for a dinosaur. Fully grown, it measured at most 3 feet 3 inches (1 m) long, much of which was tail. It weighed just over a pound (500 g), similar to a crow. However, it was not built for flight—it had short forearms instead of wings. The feathers of *Sinosauropteryx* were short and bristly, more like the down on a bird's belly than the long quills on its wings; they were useless for flight. These first feathers were probably insulation, helping the animal to keep warm and remain active. It needed to move fast to catch its prey—one fossil, also from Liaoning, was found with the remains of a lizard in its digestive tract.

Sinosauropteryx lived in the early Cretaceous period, about 125 million years ago. More recent discoveries have pushed back the record of feathered dinosaurs to the end of the preceding Jurassic period. The collective discovery of various feathered dinosaurs has shown that feathers did not evolve for flying; instead they were first useful for other things and changed their purpose later on.

Another feathered dinosaur, *Anchiornis huxleyi* lived about 160 million years ago. Although it was older than *Sinosauropteryx*, it arguably appeared more birdlike. Its front arms looked more like wings, and its feathers were longer and more like the flight feathers of modern birds. It would not have been able to fly, but it may have been able to glide.

Researchers have been able to find traces of colored pigment in the feathers of both *Sinosauropteryx* and *Anchiornis*. Their best guesses are that *Sinosauropteryx* was orangey brown with a striped tail and a bandit mask like a raccoon, while *Anchiornis* was mostly dark gray and white, but it had orange freckling on its cheeks and in a crest on top of its head. As with modern birds, such colorful plumage may have evolved to attract mates.

As dinosaurs developed into birds, they became smaller—another important step on the road to flight. *Anchiornis* was about half the size of *Sinosauropteryx*, measuring 1 foot 3¾ inches (40 cm) long, with a wingspan of 1 foot 7½ inches (50 cm)—smaller than a pigeon. But it wasn't only small dinosaurs such as *Anchiornis* and *Sinosauropteryx* that had feathers. Scientists now believe, for example, that such famous predators as *Velociraptor* and *Tyrannosaurus rex* also had feathers on at least parts of their bodies.

RIGHT: *Sinosauropteryx* was the first feathered dinosaur to be found.

Sarcosuchus

PERIOD: Cretaceous
LOCALITY: Africa, South America
SIZE: 33 ft. (10 m) long

Crocodiles have been around for more than 200 million years, and their shape hasn't changed a great deal in that time. Their size, however, has.

Sarcosuchus imperator lived about 120 million years ago. Its fossils are known from the deserts of West Africa and Brazil in South America, which at the time were adjacent regions of the giant southern continent Gondwana. And it was huge: The biggest grew more than 33 feet (10 m) long and weighed more than 8 tons. This is more than twice as long and eight times heavier than its largest living relative, the saltwater crocodile.

At this time, most crocodiles lived in the sea. The particle size of the sandstones and mudstones in which *Sarcosuchus* was found, however, show that its bones were fossilized in rivers, which is where most modern species of crocodile live.

It's one of a number of species of enormous extinct crocodiles and may have been the largest of them all. The scales of reptiles and fish can bear rings—in the same way as those in a tree trunk—showing varying growth rates caused by seasonal changes in weather and food supply. By studying the growth patterns recorded in fossil skin, scientists have estimated that *Sarcosuchus* may have taken fifty years to grow to its full size and could probably live for decades beyond that.

Some crocodile species specialize in hunting fish; others prey on land animals. Comparing the teeth of *Sarcosuchus* to living species suggests that it fell into the second group. Modern crocodiles that hunt in this way ambush their prey, lurking low in the water to get close enough to pounce.

Today's crocodiles have the strongest bite of any living animal. Once they get their teeth into something, they are almost impossible to shake off. Their ancient relatives would have been equally tenacious, and *Sarcosuchus* must have made meals of many an unwitting dinosaur that came to drink at the water's edge.

ABOVE: Placing *Sarcosuchus* (center) next to modern crocodiles gives an idea of its huge size.

Angimordella

PERIOD: Cretaceous
LOCALITY: Asia
SIZE: ⅛ in. (4 mm)

In the early days of the dinosaurs, the forests were filled with conifers and ferns. About 100 million years ago, during the Cretaceous period, the flowering plants, a group called the angiosperms, arrived in an explosive burst of evolution. Today flowering plants make up 90 percent of the approximately 350,000 living species of plants.

Writing in 1879, Charles Darwin called their sudden appearance and apparently rapid evolution an "abominable mystery." Since then, many scientists have deduced that flowering plants owe their success to their partnership with insects. Conifers are pollinated by the wind, but 90 percent of angiosperms rely on insects to carry their pollen between flowers.

Insects are by far the most diverse group of animals, with about a million species described, and probably at least a million more species remaining undiscovered. Like flowering plants, they also became common and diverse around the mid-Cretaceous, and it seems probable that the two groups played a part in each other's success.

Until 2019 the earliest evidence of insect pollination dated from about 50 million years ago. Then a team of Chinese and American researchers revealed a tiny beetle preserved in a 99-million-year-old piece of amber, with more than 60 grains of pollen from a flowering plant stuck to its body. This beetle, found in Myanmar, belonged to a new species called *Angimordella burmitina*. It was a member of a group called the tumbling flower beetles, after the erratic movements they use to escape from predators. They eat pollen and are still important pollinators today. *Angimordella* had hairs on its body that trapped pollen as it moved from flower to flower, and the pollen has ridges on its surface that would have helped it stick to insects. Even at this early date, both flowers and insects had evolved features to make pollination more effective.

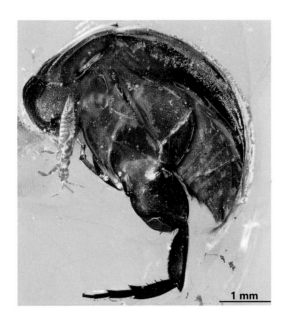

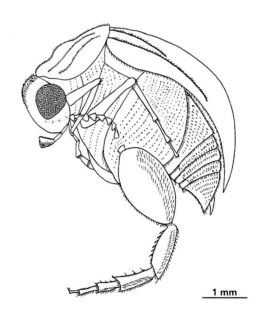

1 mm

ABOVE: Preserved in amber, *Angimordella* is the oldest known insect pollinator.

Spinosaurus

PERIOD: Cretaceous
LOCALITY: Africa
SIZE: 50 ft. (15 m) long

*S*pinosaurus aegyptiacus is sometimes described as the biggest meat-eating dinosaur of all. However, it's difficult to say precisely how large it was, because a complete specimen has not been found. But it was probably about 50 feet (15 m) long and weighed at least 7 tons—more than an elephant. Whatever the precise figures, it was a giant—similar in size or even bigger than the better-known *Tyrannosaurus rex*, which was about 40 feet (12 m) long and weighed about 8 tons.

The most obvious feature of *Spinosaurus*, which has given it its name, is the sail on its back. It was supported by bony spines growing out of its backbone and reaching as high as an adult human. Various scientists have suggested that it could have been a radiator to help the animal maintain a steady body temperature, a hump for storing food like a camel, or a flashy ornament to attract mates.

Yet another suggestion is that the sail was a kind of fin that helped *Spinosaurus* to swim. Whether or not this is true, many scientists believe that *Spinosaurus* spent much of its time in the water. Its nostrils were high on its skull, which would have helped it to breathe while in the water, and it had a long, pointed snout and teeth much like a crocodile. Chemical and fossil evidence also suggests that *Spinosaurus* ate fish, although it was probably also capable of hunting or scavenging on land.

The original specimen, found in the Egyptian desert and described in 1915, was held in the German city of Munich, where it was destroyed in an air raid during World War II. More have been found since then in the Kem Kem beds along the border between Morocco and Algeria, which were laid down by an ancient river system. *Spinosaurus* lived about 97 million years ago but died out well before the mass extinction that wiped out all dinosaurs.

RIGHT: *Spinosaurus* was one of the largest meat-eating dinosaurs.

Argentinosaurus

PERIOD: Cretaceous
LOCALITY: South America
SIZE: 100 ft. (30 m) long

The dinosaurs' heavyweight championship is a difficult contest to judge, because many of what look like the largest species are known from only a few fossil fragments—the chances of something gargantuan being neatly buried and fossilized in one piece are slim.

Argentinosaurus huinculensis, for example, is known from only a leg bone, pieces of backbone, and some ribs. But that's enough to show that it was one of the most massive animals to walk the Earth. It could grow to almost 100 feet (30 m) long and weighed 70 tons or more when fully grown. That's more than ten times the weight of the largest elephants, and about five times the weight of other well-known dinosaur giants such as *Diplodocus*. However, it may not have been the biggest; in 2014 paleontologists discovered a species they called *Patagotitan*, which they believe was even larger. Both species lived in what is now southern South America about 100 million to 90 million years ago.

Argentinosaurus, *Patagotitan*, and all the other huge dinosaurs belonged to a group of plant eaters called the sauropods. To grow to these sizes, an animal needs to eat a lot of food, especially if that food is plant matter, which, pound for pound, contains less energy than meat and takes longer to digest. It has been suggested that the secret of the sauropods' enormous bulk was their long necks, which would have enabled them to pluck food from a wide area without moving their feet, including reaching high into the trees to forage where other species could not. It also seems these dinosaurs did not chew their food, meaning they could eat more quickly.

Argentinosaurus certainly had a lot of growing to do. Newly hatched animals were only about 3 feet 3 inches (1 m) long and weighed 11 pounds (5 kg)—about the same size as a goose. This means they had to grow more than any other vertebrate to reach full size, which would have taken several decades. It's thought that at their peak growth rate they could put on about 120 pounds (55 kg) of weight every day.

The size of the largest sauropods would have kept them safe from most predators, particularly because there is also evidence that they lived in herds. Even so, there were large, meat-eating dinosaurs living in the same place at the same time, such as *Giganotosaurus*, which may have been able to prey upon these plant-eating giants.

LEFT: A reconstructed skeleton of *Argentinosaurus*, possibly the largest dinosaur of all.

FOLLOWING PAGES: *Argentinosaurus* browsed on plants and may have lived in herds.

Maiasaura
and Oviraptor

MAIASAURA
PERIOD: Cretaceous
LOCALITY: North America
SIZE: 30 ft. (9 m) long

OVIRAPTOR
PERIOD: Cretaceous
LOCALITY: Asia
SIZE: 5 ft. (1.5 m) long

Picture a nesting colony of penguins, tens of thousands of birds, squawking and squabbling, coming and going from their nests with food for their chicks. Imagine that sight with 2-ton dinosaurs instead of birds, and you'll have an idea of how *Maiasaura* lived.

Maiasaura peeblesorum was the first dinosaur to be found with evidence that it cared for its young—the name means "good mother lizard." Fossilized remains of adults, eggs, babies, and nests have given us a better picture of its family life than for any other dinosaur.

It was a member of the large group of plant-eating, duck-billed dinosaurs called the hadrosaurs. It reached about 30 feet (9 m) long and weighed a little more than 2 tons. It lived in herds that could be 10,000 strong, in what is now Montana. Its home was a dry plain, similar to the grasslands of Africa, which are now home to herds of antelope and zebra. It had no armor or defenses against predators and so probably, like these modern herbivores, relied for its safety on speed and strength in numbers.

When *Maiasaura* were breeding, they built their nests in dense crowds, so close to one another that they could have knocked each other with their tails as they turned. But instead of sitting on its

eggs, *Maiasaura* seems to have covered its nest with vegetation. This would have produced heat as it rotted, keeping the eggs warm. Some crocodiles and a few living birds do the same.

Females laid thirty to forty eggs in a brood, each about the size of an ostrich egg. The young were unable to walk when they were born,

ABOVE: Newly hatched *Maiasaura* could not walk and relied on their parents for food.

RIGHT: *Maiasaura* lived in herds and nested in colonies.

meaning that their parents had to bring them food. It was probably a year or two before the young were able to leave the nest and fend for themselves. It's thought that nine out of every ten hatchlings died during this time, being eaten by predators, trampled by neighbors, or killed by disease or bad weather. They were able to breed from the age of three and reached full size after eight years.

Oviraptor philoceratops lived at the same time as *Maiasaura*, 75 million years ago in the late Cretaceous period. Its fossils have been found on the other side of the world in Mongolia. It, too, cared for its eggs, although it seems to have sat on them, warming them with its body like most living birds. No large colonies have been found.

Oviraptor was a theropod. It was much smaller than *Maiasaura*, about 5 feet (1.5 m) long and weighing about 65 pounds (30 kg), about the size of a flightless bird such as an emu. Indeed, with its small stature and toothless, beaky mouth, *Oviraptor* would have looked birdlike. Closely related species had feathers on their bodies, tail, and arms, and *Oviraptor* was probably the same. It might have used its feathered

arms to cover its eggs in the same way that many birds use their wings.

The first fossil of *Oviraptor* was found in the 1920s by an expedition led by the American paleontologist Roy Chapman Andrews. His exploits and dinosaur discoveries in a series of expeditions to Mongolia and the Gobi Desert made him famous, and he may have inspired the fictional movie archaeologist Indiana Jones.

Andrews's team found their *Oviraptor* sitting on a pile of eggs. The scientists' first theory was that it had died in the middle of a meal—*Oviraptor* means "egg stealer." However, later discoveries of related dinosaurs also sitting on eggs showed that the animal had been nesting, not hunting. We're still not sure what *Oviraptor* did eat, although the first fossil discovered appeared to have had a lizard in its stomach.

Discoveries such as *Maiasaura* and *Oviraptor* help scientists to make sense of new fossils, and to develop new theories about old ones. As they do, the evidence is growing that many species of dinosaur had complex social lives and cared for their young.

Triceratops

PERIOD: Cretaceous
LOCALITY: North America
SIZE: 26 ft. (8 m)

I n 2011 a team of scientists from Yale University reported on the discovery of a fossil horn of a *Triceratops*, or another species like it, in mudstone from the Hell Creek Formation of Montana. These rocks were laid down just a few thousand years before the devastating meteor collision that marked the end of the Cretaceous period.

This made it the geologically most recent dinosaur found to date. It also filled a gap in the fossil record. Dinosaurs are rare in rocks formed in the last few million years of the Cretaceous; paleontologists call this the "three-meter gap" in the fossil record. Some scientists have concluded that dinosaurs were already well on the way to extinction when the meteor struck, and that while the impact might have helped finish them off, it was not the decisive cause of their demise. Finding a dinosaur fossil so close to the end of the Cretaceous was a hint that this theory was mistaken and that some dinosaurs were thriving up to the point when the meteor struck.

When the horn was found, *Triceratops* was already known to be one of the last dinosaurs. It appeared in the fossil record about 68 million years ago, less than 3 million years before the meteor impact. It's one of the final members of a group of horned dinosaur species that first appeared tens of millions of years earlier, in the Jurassic period.

Triceratops was a heavily built plant eater. It could grow to more than 26 feet (8 m) long and weighed more than 10 tons, four times heavier than a rhinoceros. *Triceratops* fossils are common—it may have been the most common, large plant-eating species of its time—but they are nearly always found on their own, suggesting that the animals did not live in herds.

There are several theories about what *Triceratops* did with its three horns and the bony frill around its neck. One possibility is that they formed a defense against predators—bite marks on fossil skeletons provide evidence that *Tyrannosaurus* attacked *Triceratops*. Another is that they were used in fights among *Triceratops* themselves, because some skulls appear to show wounds that could have been caused in this way. A further theory is that they were for show, used to attract mates rather than to repel other animals.

OPPOSITE: Skull of *Triceratops,* one of the last dinosaurs.

RIGHT: A huge asteroid struck Earth 66 million years ago, close to what is now Mexico.

Triceratops may have been the most common of the large plant eaters of its time.

4

THE RISE OF
MAMMALS

OPPOSITE: *Arsinotherium*, one of dozens of species of
extinct rhinoceroses.

PERIOD	PERIOD
PALEOGENE	NEOGENE
EPOCH	EPOCH
PALEOCENE (66–56 million years ago)	MIOCENE (23–5.3 million years ago)
EOCENE (56–34 million years ago)	PLIOCENE (5.3–2.6 million years ago)
OLIGOCENE (34–23 million years ago)	

The asteroid that killed the dinosaurs cloaked Earth in darkness. However, most mammals were nocturnal and had been living in darkness all along. They were also relatively small, meaning they didn't need much food, and many of them lived in burrows. They were therefore well equipped to survive the hellish conditions that followed the asteroid impact. When the smoke cleared, they came into their own.

Over the next 10 million years, mammals evolved in size. This was the era of the biggest land mammals in Earth's history. There were rhinoceroses and elephants bigger than any surviving today, along with huge sloths, rodents, and many others. Some mammals took to the trees, with primates evolving the grasping hands and forward-facing eyes that humans would eventually inherit. Other mammals returned to the seas, where they would eventually grow into the largest animals of all time. Additional mammals also took to the air, making bats the fourth group of animals (after insects, pterosaurs, and birds) to have evolved flight.

BELOW: The earliest members of the horse family were far smaller than today's horses.

OPPOSITE: The elephant *Deinotherium* weighed twice as much as its modern relatives.

As the millennia passed, the landmasses drifted farther apart, each one an ark carrying its own cargo of animals and plants. In Australia and South America, marsupials ruled. In Eurasia, Africa, and North America, the placental mammals held sway.

The continents did not stay isolated. Cooling climates locked up water in ice caps and caused sea levels to fall, opening land bridges between North America and Europe as well as between Asia and North America. Elephants and rhinoceroses traveled from Africa to Asia to North America; horses moved in the opposite direction, from North America into Asia. These connections opened up new territories for some species and spelled doom for others.

Three million years ago, a more permanent land bridge was created between North and South America, when colliding tectonic plates threw up volcanic islands, linking the two continents. This began a process called the Great American Interchange, as plants and animals moved from one continent to the other. Migrants from the north were more successful; today about half of South America's mammals are descended from northern ancestors, whereas only a few species, such as armadillos and opossums, made the journey from south to north.

RIGHT: Print from 1862 shows the giant armadillo *Glyptodon* (left) and sloth *Megatherium*.

Purgatorius

PERIOD: Paleogene
EPOCH: Paleocene
DISTRIBUTION: North America
SIZE: 6 in. (15 cm) long

Many of the mammals that survived through the end of the Cretaceous period looked like *Purgatorius*—in other words, like small rodents. However, *Purgatorius* was not a true rodent—it was the oldest known primate, the group that includes lemurs, monkeys, apes, and humans. It lived 65 million years ago and was given its name from Purgatory Hill in Montana, where it was found in deposits laid down soon after the dinosaurs became extinct.

For decades, *Purgatorius* was known from only fossil teeth and fragments of jaw. These remnants indicated that it was the size of a large mouse and ate insects and fruit. Its teeth also revealed that it was more closely related to primates than to rodents, shrews, or any of the other animals it might superficially resemble.

Modern primates are well adapted for life in the trees. With only fossilized teeth to go on, it was not possible to know if the same was true of *Purgatorius*, or whether it was a ground dweller. In 2015, however, scientists described fossils of ankle bones belonging to *Purgatorius*, collected in the same locations as the original remains. These were the ankles of a tree dweller; they were flexible and able to support grasping, adjustable hands. The find suggested that primates moved to the trees early in their history, perhaps climbing to reach the fruit from the many tree species that were evolving around the same time.

BELOW: *Purgatorius* is the earliest known primate.

Barylambda

PERIOD: Paleogene
EPOCH: Paleocene
DISTRIBUTION: North America
SIZE: 8 ft. (2.5 m) long

When the dinosaurs disappeared, they left a vacancy for large animals. For a herbivore, being big had advantages, because a large stomach and a long digestive tract can extract more nutrients from plant food. Being large also helps combat predators.

The pantodonts, a group of browsing herbivores, were among the first mammals to grow large. They initially appeared in what is now China soon after the dinosaurs became extinct and lasted for 30 million years. Their time on Earth coincided with a period when the climate was much warmer than today, with forests growing near both of the poles. They were widely distributed; Pantodont teeth have been found in Antarctica in the south, and their footprints have been found on the Norwegian island of Svalbard in the north.

The smallest pantodonts were the size of a dog and weighed about 22 pounds (10 kg). *Barylambda*, which lived from about 60 million to 50 million years ago, was at the other end of the scale. At 8 feet (2.5 m) long and weighing more than 1,400 pounds (650 kg)—similar to a bison—it was one of the largest pantodonts and one of the biggest animals of its time. Its fossils are known from Wyoming and Colorado, making it a successor of the herbivorous dinosaurs that lived in the same locality a few million years earlier. Heavily built, it might have used its thick tail as a prop, enabling it to rear up on its hind legs to reach leaves high up in the trees.

BELOW: *Barylambda* was one of the first large herbivores to evolve after the dinosaurs' extinction.

PERIOD: Paleogene
EPOCH: Paleocene
DISTRIBUTION: South America
SIZE: 43 ft. (13 m) long

Titanoboa

*T*itanoboa was a 43-foot (13-m)-long snake that weighed more than 2,425 pounds (1,100 kg). That is twice as long as the longest living snake, the reticulated python, and fifteen times heavier than the world's heaviest snake, the anaconda. *Titanoboa* was the largest land vertebrate of its time, the biggest snake in history, and the largest predator on Earth for 10 million years.

It was discovered in the Cerrejón coal deposits of northeastern Colombia. These contain exceptionally well-preserved fossil remains from what may have been the world's first tropical rain forest, dating from 60 million years ago.

The size of cold-blooded animals, such as snakes, depends on the climate. The warmer it is, the bigger they can grow. The paleontologists who discovered *Titanoboa* calculated that a snake of its size could have survived only in a climate several degrees hotter than today, and ancient climate records confirm their estimate.

As well as being hotter, the tropical forest was much wetter than today's, receiving nearly 13 feet (4 m) of rainfall each year, twice as much as the current rainfall in the Amazon. While *Titanoboa* was the biggest beast in this lush and swampy habitat, it wasn't the only outsize creature; it lived alongside large turtles, crocodiles, and fish.

Judging by its many closely packed teeth, *Titanoboa* was adapted to hunt fish. This is unknown in today's boa constrictors—the living species most closely related to *Titanoboa*—although anacondas are known to catch fish and also caiman, the alligator of South America. In fact, they will eat most creatures big or small, and *Titanoboa* may have been equally willing to crush and swallow anything it could wrap and coil itself around.

125

LEFT: *Titanoboa* was the biggest snake in evolutionary history.

Gastornis and Phorusrhacos

GASTORNIS
PERIOD: Paleogene
EPOCH: Paleocene–Eocene
DISTRIBUTION: Europe, Asia, North America
SIZE: 6 ft. 6 in. (2 m) tall

PHORUSRHACOS
PERIOD: Neogene
EPOCH: Miocene
DISTRIBUTION: South America
SIZE: 8 ft. (2.5 m) tall

Looking at these two enormous birds, you might think that they continued just where the dinosaurs left off—they look like feathered dinosaurs.

Gastornis lived during the Eocene epoch, 55 million to 40 million years ago. It was the largest European animal of its time; its fossils were first discovered in the suburbs of Paris in 1855. Closely related species have also been found in China and North America. It is not known how *Gastornis* crossed the Atlantic, although there were periods when land bridges connected the continents.

The largest species stood more than 6 feet 6 inches (2 mt) tall and weighed 375 pounds (170 kg), making it a little shorter than an ostrich but somewhat heavier. Like all the largest birds, it would have been flightless. As improbable as it may seem, its skeleton shows that its closest living relatives are ducks and geese.

Gastornis had an ax-like beak that has led many to believe it was a predator, but recently that view has changed. Birds of prey have hooked beaks, but *Gastornis* had a straight beak that scientists now think was adapted for eating fruit and cracking seeds like an enormous finch. Analysis of the chemical composition of its bones has also shown that *Gastornis* fed on plants.

If *Gastornis* was an herbivore, it leaves terror birds, such as *Phorusrhacos*, as the undisputed champions of deadly giant birds.

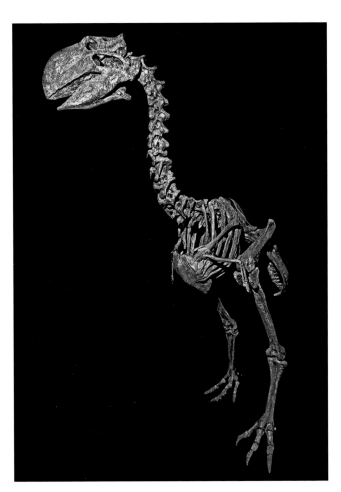

Fig. 1. Restauration du squelette de *Gastornis Edwardsii*, oiseau éocène

FAR LEFT: Skeleton of *Gastornis gigantea.*

LEFT: A nineteenth-century illustration of *Gastornis parisiensis*, discovered in France in 1855.

RIGHT: Scientists believe that *Gastornis* was a plant eater.

Terror birds appeared in South America 60 million years ago, soon after the dinosaurs became extinct, and evolved to fill the gaps left by meat-eating dinosaurs. Most species were 3 feet 3 inches (1 m) tall or less, but the largest could reach 10 feet (3 m) in height. *Phorusrhacos*, which lived during the Miocene epoch, about 20 million years ago, was one of the largest, similar to an ostrich in both height and weight at 8 feet (2.5 m) tall and nearly 300 pounds (130 kg).

Terror birds certainly did have hooked beaks, along with dangerous talons. Some species would have been able to run at nearly 30 miles per hour (50 km/h)—as fast as an ostrich, and with enough speed to run down a deer or a goat. Other bulkier species would have ambushed their prey instead of chasing it.

It's not known why *Gastornis* and the terror birds became extinct, but one possibility is that they were displaced by mammals. Plant-eating mammals got gradually larger through this period, providing greater competition for *Gastornis*. The terror birds survived for much longer. No mammal in South America could match them, and their reign as the continent's top predator ended just a few million years ago. They were the only carnivorous species to successfully make the journey from South to North America after the continents became connected about 3 million years ago, and they became extinct a million years after making the journey north.

OPPOSITE: Terror birds were South America's top predators for millions of years.

BELOW: *Phorusrhacos* had a hooked beak that was perfect for tearing flesh.

PERIOD: Paleogene
EPOCH: Eocene
DISTRIBUTION: North America
SIZE: 2 ft. (60 cm) long

Sifrhippus

Horses are large, strong, and fast—superbly adapted for life on grasslands. The first horses, however, were substantially different.

Sifrhippus sandrae, the oldest known member of the family, lived in forests in Wyoming 55 million years ago. It was a browser, feeding on the leaves of trees and bushes instead of on grass. And at only 11 to 13 pounds (5–6 kg), it was the size of a domestic cat.

Over millions of years, the descendants of *Sifrhippus* became more like the horses we see today. Their toes fused into hooves, ideal for running long distances over hard ground, and their teeth adapted to eat grass. They also grew larger—today's wild horses can reach more than 1,100 pounds (500 kg).

Early in its history, however, *Sifrhippus* became smaller. It evolved during a time of climate change, when a huge increase in atmospheric carbon dioxide sent temperatures rising by 9 degrees Fahrenheit (5°C) or more. Body size and temperature are closely linked. While reptiles grow bigger in warm climates, warm-blooded animals risk overheating and so tend to be smaller, or to have adaptations for cooling down, such as the ears of an elephant. Fossils of *Sifrhippus* show that over a period of 130,000 years its body weight shrank by about one-third as the world warmed, and then it returned to its original size when it cooled again over the next 45,000 years.

There are hundreds of species of extinct horses. But all living horses, zebras, and donkeys are descended from a species called *Dinohippus* that lived just 4 million years ago. *Dinohippus* lived in North America, but America's original wild horses became extinct 10,000 years ago, through a combination of climate change and hunting by humans. The mustangs that roam North America today are descended from the horses introduced by European colonists in the sixteenth century.

RIGHT: The oldest known horse, *Sifrihippus*, was the size of a domestic cat.

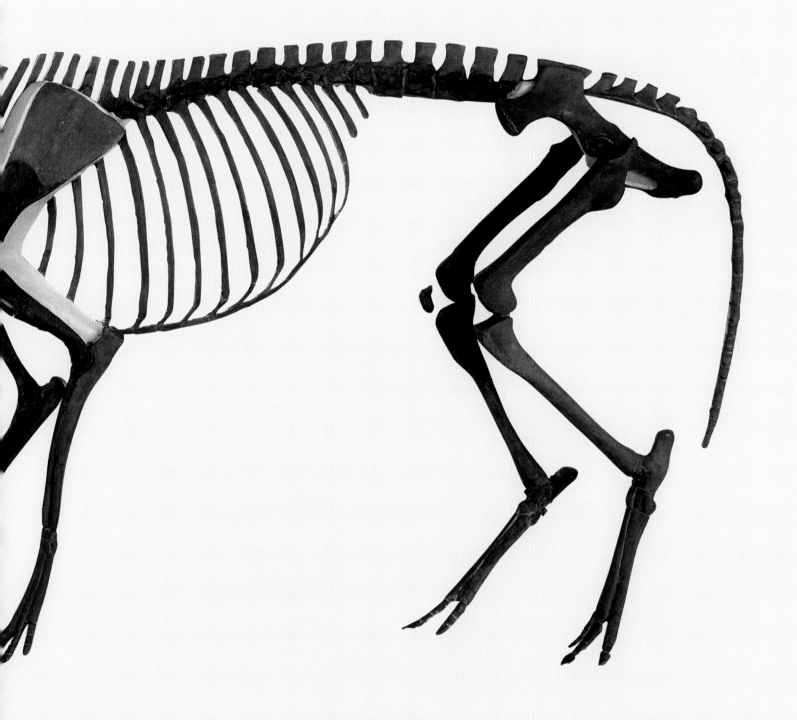

Mesonyx and Daeodon

MESONYX
PERIOD: Paleogene
EPOCH: Eocene
DISTRIBUTION: Asia,
North America
SIZE: 5 ft. (1.5 m) long

DAEODON
PERIOD: Paleogene–Neogene
EPOCH: Oligocene–Miocene
DISTRIBUTION: North America
SIZE: 6 ft. 6 in. (2 m) tall

*M*esonyx was a meat eater. It looked similar to a wolf and was a similar size. Like wolves, it would have been a swift runner, but it chased down its prey on hooves instead of paws. Today we think of the hoofed mammals called ungulates, such as sheep and antelopes, as grazers and browsers. However, 60 million years ago, some of them developed a taste for flesh.

Mesonyx belongs to a group of carnivorous ungulates called the mesonychids. Fossils show that they originated in China and spread to North America.

The smallest species of mesonychid were similar in size to a fox; the biggest were the size of a bear. All had the long, sharp canines characteristic of carnivores, while the back teeth that plant-eating ungulates use to grind up their food were adapted for slicing meat.

Mesonychids were one of several groups of meat-eating ungulates that lived between 60 million and 10 million years ago. The entelodonts are another example. They are sometimes called hell pigs, but they are more closely related to hippopotamuses and whales.

The entelodonts lived from 37 million to 16 million years ago. They originated in Asia and spread to Europe and North America. *Daeodon*, which lived between 29 million and 19 million years ago, was the largest, standing more than 6 feet 6 inches (2 m) tall. It had a skull like a pig and a body built like a bison, with slender legs and cloven hooves that would have made it a fast runner. *Daeodon* fossils have been found across the United States, from Oregon to Florida and from California to New Jersey.

OPPOSITE: *Mesonyx* was a carnivore related to sheep and antelopes.

ABOVE: With hooves and sharp teeth, entelodonts are sometimes called hell pigs.

BELOW: Skeleton of *Entelodon major*, from central Asia.

FOLLOWING PAGES: *Andrewsarchus*, known from a single skull, may have been one of the largest meat-eating mammals.

Despite their sharp teeth, entelodonts lack the slicing teeth seen in all mammals that hunt their prey. This suggests that they were probably omnivores like pigs, willing to eat most things, and that any meat they ate was probably scavenged instead of hunted. Their large teeth may have also been used in displays and fighting; some entelodont skulls show injuries that may have been inflicted by other entelodonts.

A carnivorous ungulate related to the entelodonts called *Andrewsarchus* is known from a single fossil skull more than 2 feet 6 inches (80 cm) long and 1 foot 7½ inches (50 cm) wide. If the rest of the animal was similarly proportioned, it would have been the size of a rhinoceros, potentially making it the largest meat-eating land mammal of all time.

Today's dominant order of meat-eating mammals, the Carnivora, began as ferret-size animals living alongside bigger meat eaters such as the mesonychids and entelodonts. Starting about 40 million years ago, they began to take over. Carnivora now covers about 300 species, including cats, dogs, bears, hyenas, seals, and weasels.

PERIOD: Paleogene
EPOCH: Eocene
DISTRIBUTION: North America
SIZE: 5½ in. (14 cm) long, wingspan 1 ft. 2½ in. (37 cm)

Icaronycteris

Bats are one of the most successful groups of mammals, with more than 12,000 known species. They are found on every continent except Antarctica. The secret to their success is that they are the only mammals that can fly. Combine this with their ability to navigate in the dark by echolocation, and you have a creature well adapted for hunting the vast number of airborne insects at night.

Icaronycteris index is the oldest known bat. It lived 51 million years ago and is known from beautiful fossils discovered in the Green River Formation of western Wyoming, in rocks made up of petrified lake sediments and volcanic ash. It was 5½ inches (14 cm) long, with a wingspan of 1 foot 2½ inches (37 cm), about the size of a thrush. These dimensions put it in the middle of the size range for modern bats, which have wingspans from 6 inches (15 cm) to 5 feet (1.5 m).

Apart from its long tail, *Icaronycteris* would not look out of place alongside today's bats. Its wings indicate that it was a strong flier, and its teeth suggest that it ate insects, although it probably picked them off trees instead of catching them on the wing. Comparisons of its skull and ears with modern bats show that it was able to use echolocation.

This specialized anatomy points to undiscovered missing links between *Icaronycteris* and its nonflying ancestors. Scientists believe that these undiscovered "proto-bats" must have been tree-dwelling, nocturnal, insect-eating species, somewhat like shrews. They probably first evolved the ability to glide on flaps of skin between their limbs, like flying squirrels, and later developed the ability to fly.

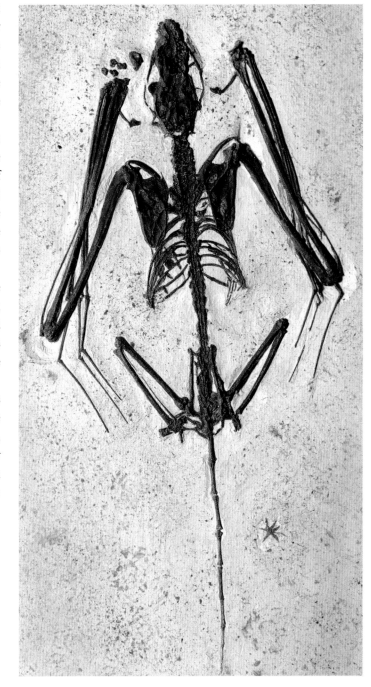

OPPOSITE: The oldest known bat, *Icaronycteris*, would have been a strong flier.

RIGHT: *Icaronycteris* is known from beautifully preserved fossils found in Wyoming.

Ambulocetus and Basilosaurus

AMBULOCETUS
PERIOD: Paleogene
EPOCH: Eocene
DISTRIBUTION: Asia
SIZE: 11 ft. 6 in. (3.5 m) long

BASILOSAURUS
PERIOD: Paleogene
EPOCH: Eocene
DISTRIBUTION: North America
SIZE: 50–65 ft. (15–20 m) long

I t's been known since Darwin's time that whales are descended from land-living mammals. But because whales are so unlike any land mammal, it has been difficult to determine which mammals these could possibly be.

DNA evidence shows that the whales' closest living, land-dwelling relative is the hippopotamus. The extinct ancestors of whales, however, looked nothing like them.

Ambulocetus natans was one such ancestor. It was one in a line of half a dozen animals whose fossils, found in India and Pakistan, show how whales began as small, deerlike animals that waded in streams, slowly evolving into oceangoing predators the length of a bus. It was a process that took 10 million years.

Ambulocetus—the name means "walking whale"—shows a key point along that evolutionary journey. It was the first marine species in the line, living 49 million years ago in coastal shallow seas and brackish river estuaries. It was large, weighing about 400 pounds (180 kg) or more—about the size of a male sea lion—and probably spent all of its time in the water, swimming with its back legs and tail like an otter. With its long snout, sharp teeth and eyes placed high on its head, it would have resembled a furry crocodile, and it probably hunted like one, drifting up on its prey until it was close enough to pounce.

Basilosaurus cetoides, which lived 41 million years ago, shows the completion of whales' journey to the sea. Its front legs were flippers, and its back legs were too small to bear its weight. It had a fluke on

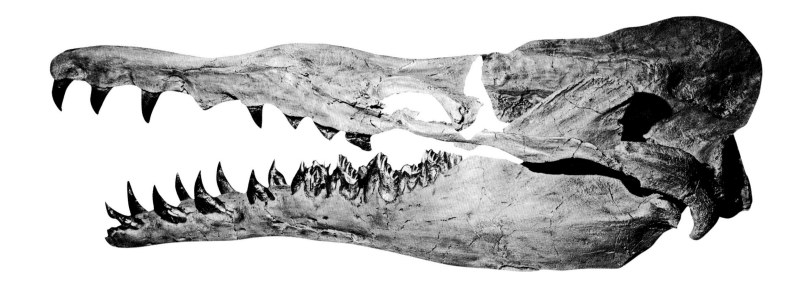

ABOVE: Skull of *Basilosaurus*, an extinct whale with the strongest jaws of any mammal.

BELOW: *Basilosaurus* probably swam by flexing its long body like an eel.

its tail and a blowhole on its head; it couldn't have left the water even if it had wanted to. The first fossils of *Basilosaurus* were found in Louisiana in 1834. They were originally thought to be from a dinosaur, which is why the animal's name means "king lizard."

Basilosaurus was as long as a sperm whale, reaching 50 to 65 feet (15–20 m), but far lighter, weighing about 5 tons, compared with 40 tons for its modern relative. It probably swam by flexing its slim body like an eel, and it was a powerful predator, hunting fish, sharks, and other whales. Scientists have calculated that it had the most powerful jaws of any mammal. Damage to the skulls of other fossil whales show how it first seized its prey with its front teeth and then maneuvered it into position farther back for the killing bite.

Reaching the sea was not the end of the whales' evolutionary journey. About 30 million years ago, the line split into the toothed whales, including dolphins, orcas, and sperm whales, and the baleen whales, such as the humpback and blue whales, which evolved into the largest animals known.

OPPOSITE: *Ambulocetus* was the first whale ancestor to live in the sea.

ABOVE: Fossil bones of *Basilosaurus* at a site in Egypt.

PERIOD: Paleogene
EPOCH: Oligocene
DISTRIBUTION: Asia, Europe
SIZE: 23 ft. (7m) long, 16 ft. 6 in. (5 m) tall

Paraceratherium

The extinct rhinoceros *Paraceratherium* was more than 23 feet (7 m) long and about 16 feet 6 inches (5 m) high at the shoulder. Its long neck would have made it taller still, able to reach higher than a giraffe. The largest individuals weighed 15 to 20 tons. That made it about twice as long and three times as heavy as an African elephant. It also made it a strong contender for one of the largest land mammals to have lived.

Paraceratherium lived in the Oligocene, from 34 million to 23 million years ago. It has been found from Eastern Europe to China in habitats ranging from desert to forest. It was a browser and would have ranged over large areas to find the hundreds of pounds of food it needed each day to survive.

Bones of *Paraceratherium* have been found bearing the toothmarks of giant crocodiles of a similar size. These marks show that it was not entirely safe from predators, although crocodiles would have targeted young or sick animals instead of trying to tackle a healthy adult.

Rhinoceroses date back 50 million years and have evolved into different forms. Some lived in the water like hippopotamuses; others had two horns positioned side by side on their noses instead of the front-to-back arrangement seen in today's species; some were fast runners; and others lived in the mountains and sported woolly coats.

It's not known why *Paraceratherium* became extinct. One possibility is that they could not compete for food with elephants, whose trunks make them extremely efficient foragers. Today's five rhinoceros species are desperately endangered by poaching and, like *Paraceratherium*, could also become lost animals all too soon.

143

LEFT: The size of *Paraceratherium* can be gauged against the wolf-size carnivore *Hyaenodon*.

Chalicotherium

PERIOD: Neogene
EPOCH: Miocene
DISTRIBUTION: Europe, Asia
SIZE: 8 ft. (2.5 m) tall

Today's large plant-eating mammals, from rhinoceroses to deer, all have similar body shapes: four legs of equal length that are good for running and a horizontal body. They obtain food by reaching with their necks down to the ground or up into trees.

Chalicotherium shows that this was not the only way to be a large herbivore. It was an ungulate, related to horses and rhinoceroses. And it was big—as tall as an Asian elephant when standing on all fours, and as heavy as a rhinoceros weighing in at more than 3,300 pounds (1,500 kg). However, with a head like a horse, a body like a gorilla, and claws like a sloth, it looked nothing like today's ungulates. *Chalicotherium*'s long claws and long front legs—much longer than its back legs—would have made it incapable of galloping. Instead it would have walked on its knuckles much like an ape or a chimpanzee.

Those claws would have helped to fend off predators, and they would have come into their own when the animal fed. The patterns of wear on its skeleton reveal that it sat back on its haunches and reached high into the trees with its front legs, using its claws to grasp and strip plant material.

This particular species, *Chalicotherium goldfussi*, appeared in the fossil record about 15 million years ago. The first specimens were found near the German city of Frankfurt in the 1830s. Paleontologists now know that it was one of a group of related species with the same body shape that lived in Europe, Asia, and Africa from about 30 million years ago until approximately 4 million years ago.

LEFT: *Chalicotherium* walked on its knuckles like an ape.

Nyanzapithecus alesi

PERIOD: Neogene
EPOCH: Miocene
DISTRIBUTION: Africa
SIZE: unknown

Dozens of fossil ape species are known from Africa, Asia, and Europe. However, because they lived in forests, where dead animals are rarely buried in sediments, most of them are known only from teeth or fragments of jaw. The oldest fossil ape, for example, a 25-million-year-old species discovered in Tanzania, is known from a single jawbone.

That is why the discovery of the well-preserved skull of a 13-million-year-old ape, announced in 2017, made headlines, especially because it was the first from around the time that the group containing the apes and humans split from the rest of the primates. This fossil ape, in other words, has offered a clue to what the ancestors of modern apes looked like, and it has provided evidence that all apes are descended from an ancient African species.

The skull, belonging to a new species christened *Nyanzapithecus alesi*, was discovered in northern Kenya. John Ekusi, the Kenyan fossil hunter who found it, nicknamed it Alesi, which means "ancestor" in the local Turkana language. The skull came from a 16-month-old infant, still with its milk teeth. The shape of its teeth indicate that it was an ape instead of a monkey.

Had he or she lived, Alesi would have weighed about 25 pounds (11 kg). That's the same as a medium-size monkey, although this ape would have more closely resembled a gibbon. However, the inner ear of Alesi's skull—the organ used for balance—along with the fossil arm bone of a closely related species, show that these apes would not have been nearly as agile as gibbons. Instead of swinging beneath the branches, Alesi would have walked along them.

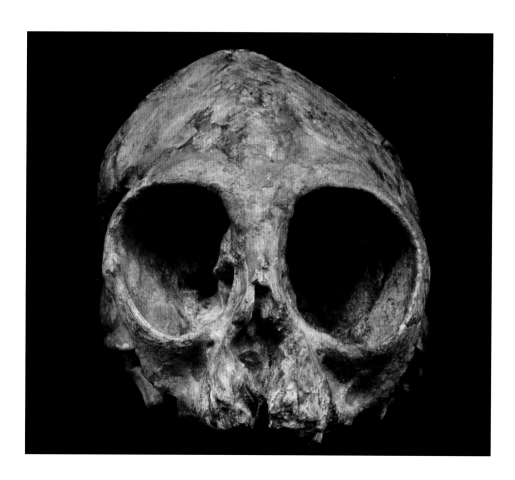

RIGHT: This fossil ape, nicknamed Alesi, was sixteen months old when it died.

Thylacosmilus

PERIOD: Neogene
EPOCH: Miocene–Pliocene
DISTRIBUTION: South America
SIZE: 5 ft. (1.5 m) long

This mammal was not a saber-toothed cat; it was more like a saber-toothed marsupial. *Thylacosmilus* hunted in the forests of South America between 10 million and 3 million years ago. It's no longer classed as a true marsupial but instead as a member of a related extinct group. Its name, which means "pouch saber," is a good description; a baby *Thylacosmilus* would have spent its early life safe in its mother's pouch.

Today Australia is the last stronghold of marsupials, but DNA evidence points to them having originated in South America 130 million years ago and migrating to Australia while the two continents were joined in the southern supercontinent Gondwana.

Thylacosmilus weighed about 220 pounds (100 kg), similar to the jaguars that hunt in South American rain forests today. Its legs show that it relied on stealth, not speed, to catch its prey.

Unlike cats, which kill with the strength of their bite, it had weak jaws. Instead it would have held its prey down with its legs before plunging its saber teeth into a soft part such as the throat.

Thylacosmilus offers an excellent example of what's called convergent evolution, showing how different species can evolve similar traits. While it shares hugely enlarged canines with the saber-toothed cats, the two animals were otherwise substantially different. The shape of the skull of *Thylacosmilus*, for example, is more like a dog's than a cat's.

It was once thought that *Thylacosmilus* became extinct when carnivores entered South America from the north, after the two continents joined, about 3 million years ago. However, while northern invaders may have driven many South American marsupials to extinction, fossils reveal that *Thylacosmilus* disappeared before the saber-toothed cats arrived.

LEFT: The saber-toothed marsupial *Thylacosmilus* lived in South America.

Phoberomys

PERIOD: Neogene
EPOCH: Miocene
DISTRIBUTION: South America
SIZE: 10 ft. (3 m) long

Rodents are arguably the most successful living mammals. Of the 4,000 mammal species, 1,500 are rodents. They live on every continent except Antarctica, and many species have adapted so well to living with humans that they have become pests.

They are not, however, large. The biggest living species, the capybara of South America, is just over 3 feet 3 inches (1 m) long and weighs about 90 pounds (40 kg). That's not tiny—it's the same size as a sheep—but it's still not huge.

In the past rodents were much bigger. *Phoberomys* was 10 feet (3 m) long and weighed more than 1,500 pounds (700 kg). That's the size of a cow. It lived, probably in herds, in the rivers and swamps of eastern Venezuela about 5 million years ago.

Phoberomys had much in common with today's capybaras, which live alongside rivers and are strong swimmers. Both are members of a South American group of rodents that also includes guinea pigs. The teeth of *Phoberomys* show that it ate grass, and, judging from its discovery in rocks laid down in the ancient Orinoco Delta, it also spent much of its time in water.

Rodents may have grown large in South America because they had few other herbivores to compete with. But when the continents of North and South America joined 3 million years ago, a host of predators moved south. This probably spelled the end for *Phoberomys*, which was too big to burrow to safety and too slow to run away.

Phoberomys is not the only extinct large rodent. In 2008 a fossil skull of a rodent that may have weighed more than 2,200 pounds (1,000 kg) was discovered in Uruguay. This animal, christened *Josephoartigasia*, is the current rodent record holder.

RIGHT: Related to guinea pigs, *Phoberomys* was one of the largest rodents.

5

THE ARRIVAL
OF HUMANS

OPPOSITE: Early humans, such as *Ardipithecus ramidus*,
were at home in the trees and on the ground.

There is a famous image of human evolution showing the stages between an apelike ancestor and a modern person. They walk in a line, each a little more upright and slightly less hairy than the one behind. This is wrong.

In reality species did not follow in succession from one to the next. They lived alongside and bred with one another. Today it might feel strange to think that we shared Earth with other species of humans, but for most of human history, that is exactly how it has been.

We are descended from apes that lived in the tropical forests of Africa. However, fossils from the earliest stages of human history are rare. The oldest human, *Sahelanthropus*, is known from a single skull. The next oldest, *Orrorin tugenensis*, is known only from some teeth and fragments of jaw and limb bones.

Partly due to this shortage of evidence, we still don't understand how ancient humans are related to and descended from each another. Regardless, we now know that Africa—

LEFT: The Cradle of Humankind World Heritage site in South Africa.

OPPOSITE: The Taung child skull, a three-year-old member of *Australopithecus africanus*.

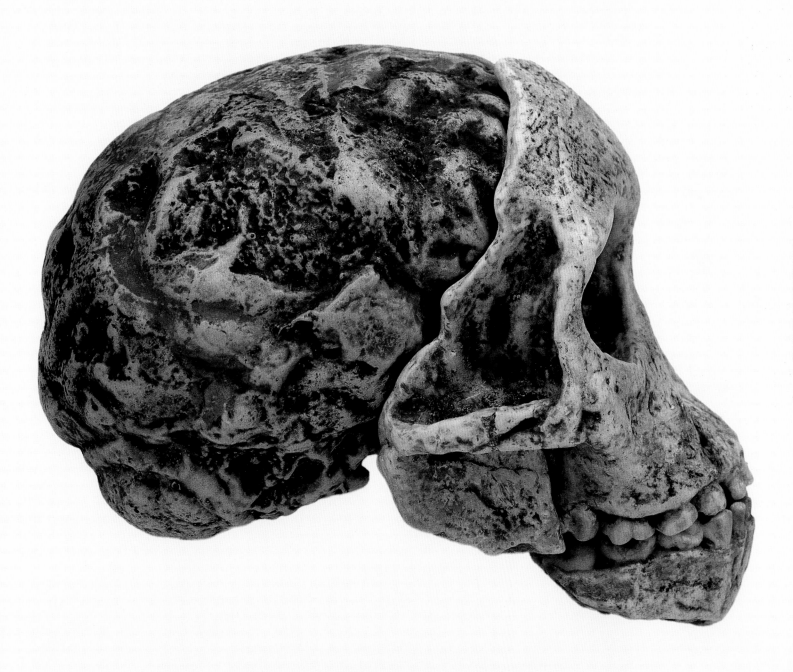

not Asia, as was thought for decades—is the cradle of humanity, and that ancient humans evolved to walk upright on two legs before they evolved large brains. We are learning how humans began to make tools, eat meat, use fire, create art, and move outward from Africa and around the world.

Many of the biggest changes in human history happened at the same time as changes in climate. Species that lived on plains instead of in woodlands, for example, appeared during a period of cooler, drier climate that caused forests to shrink and grasslands to expand.

In the past 30 years, DNA taken from ancient remains has given scientists another window into the human past. This technology has helped us better identify ancient humans and understand how they are related. It has also enabled us to see the traces of these ancient species in our own DNA.

We now know that about 2 percent of the DNA of people with European and Asian ancestry is inherited from Neanderthals; for people of African descent, the figure is 0.5 percent. The DNA of Denisovans is also visible in Aboriginal humans living in Papua New Guinea, Australia, and the Pacific Islands.

By the time humans left Africa, they were skilled toolmakers and hunters, good at working together. In Africa their prey had a chance to learn to live alongside them, and this is where today's largest land animals survive.

As humans migrated, however, they came across many animals that had not learned to fear or avoid them. In every continent outside Africa, large animals started to disappear around the time that humans arrived.

Hunting by humans may not have been the only influence on the demise of these species—changing climate may also have weakened them—but it was certainly a factor. In this chapter, we'll meet one species from Asia, Australia, and North and South America that became extinct around the time that humans arrived in these continents, plus one—the woolly mammoth—that held on for much longer.

LEFT: Substantial fossil skeletons of *Australopithecus sediba* were found in a cave.

OPPOSITE: Stone axes from Kenya made by *Homo erectus* about a million years ago.

Sahelanthropus tchadensis

PERIOD: Neogene
EPOCH: Miocene
DISTRIBUTION: Central Africa
SIZE: Unknown

*S*ahelanthropus tchadensis lived 7 million years ago. That makes it the oldest known candidate for a member of the human family. This species is identified from a skull discovered in the central African country of Chad in 2001. It was dubbed Toumaï, which means "hope of life" in the region's Dazaga language.

Toumaï lived close to the time when the human lineage split from the other great apes, and the skull shows an intriguing mixture of human and apelike features. On the ape side, Toumaï had a brain smaller than a chimpanzee's, a sloping face like a chimpanzee, and a heavy brow ridge like a gorilla. With no other confirmed remains, we can't be sure how big Toumaï was, but about the size of chimpanzee is probably a reasonable guess. Toumaï's teeth, however, resemble those of a modern human, lacking the long canines seen in apes. The

spinal cord also inserts into a hole in the base of the skull. This points to Toumaï having walked upright on two legs, because animals that walk on all fours have the hole in the back of the skull. Scientists are still debating what this complex evidence says about where Toumaï belongs on the tree of life—on the human branch, the ape branch, or a branch of its own?

As well as pushing back the history of the earliest humans, Toumaï widened the area they lived in. Previous discoveries had centered on eastern and southern Africa, thousands of miles from where Toumaï lived. The site where it was found is now desert, but when Toumaï was alive it was wooded savanna, dotted with lakes and streams, and home to extinct species of elephants, giraffes, horses, and crocodiles, to name just a few.

154

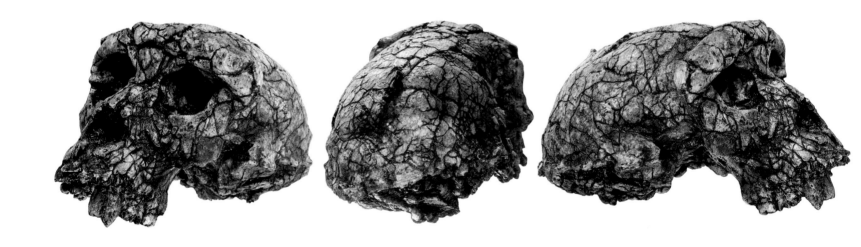

ABOVE: *Sahelanthropus* is the oldest known member of the human family.

Ardipithecus ramidus

PERIOD: Neogene
EPOCH: Pliocene
DISTRIBUTION: East Africa
SIZE: 4 ft. (1.2 m)

Meet Ardi. At 4.4 million years old, she's the oldest extinct human for whom we have a fairly complete skeleton. Ardi belongs to a species known as *Ardipithecus ramidus*. She was about the same size as a chimpanzee, weighing 110 pounds (50 kg), and her brain was also the size of a chimpanzee's. Her face, however, was flatter than a chimpanzee's and, like the older *Sahelanthropus*, she lacked long canine teeth. Her wrists were flexible, which means she would not have walked on her knuckles in the same way as modern apes.

Another difference between *Ardipithecus* and chimpanzees is that males and females are about the same size, suggesting that their social lives may have relied more on cooperation and less on settling disagreements through physical force.

The biggest differences are that she had a rigid foot as well as a hip and backbone shaped more like a human's than a chimpanzee's. These suggest that she walked upright, but her big toes were long, flexible, and stuck out like thumbs, showing that she was also able to grasp things with her feet, as apes do.

Ardi, in other words, could both walk and climb, making her well adapted for her home in central Ethiopia, which was woodland at the time she lived. The shape and chemical composition of teeth show that *Ardipithecus* was a forager, eating nuts, fruit, and roots. Ardi offers compelling evidence that upright walking evolved in the forest, long before humans moved out onto open grasslands.

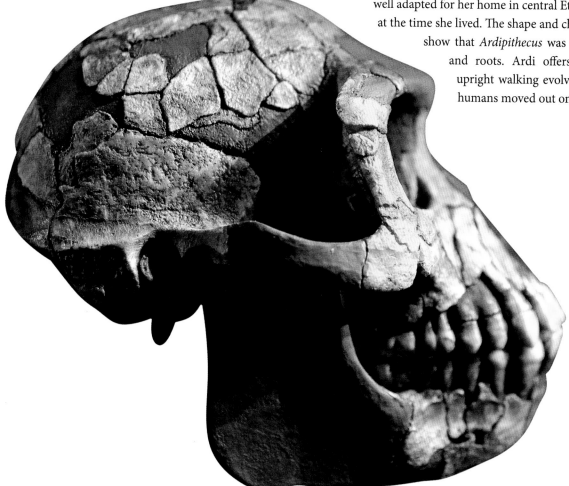

LEFT: Ardi had a chimp-size brain but more humanlike teeth.

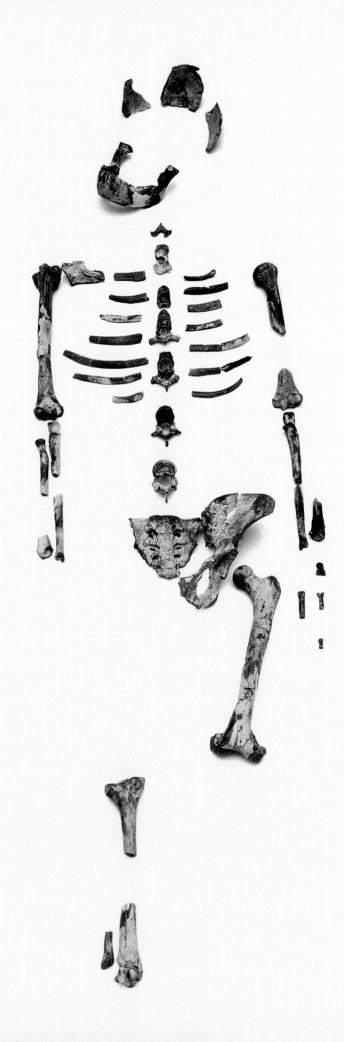

Australopithecus afarensis

PERIOD: Neogene
EPOCH: Pliocene
DISTRIBUTION: East Africa
SIZE: Males 5 ft. (1.5 m), females 3 ft. 6 in. (1.05 m)

Lucy is perhaps the most famous individual among all fossil humans. She was discovered in November 1974 in the Afar region of northern Ethiopia; her species name means "southern ape from afar." Her nickname comes from the Beatles' song "Lucy in the Sky with Diamonds," which the scientists who discovered her were playing in their camp at the time. Ethiopians call the fossil Dinkinesh, which means "you are marvelous" in the Amharic language.

Lucy is 3.2 million years old. *Australopithecus afarensis*, the species to which she belongs, lived from about 3.9 million to 2.9 million years ago. Many aspects of her anatomy, including her arched feet and the positioning of her knees, pelvis, and spine, are more similar to humans than apes, showing that she walked upright. The oldest known footprints of a bipedal ancient human—tracks made in Laetoli, Tanzania, 3.6 million years ago—were probably made by *A. afarensis*.

As well as being bipedal, Lucy had long, strong arms and curved fingers that would have been good for climbing trees. Like an ape, she had strong jaws and a big stomach, suggesting that she ate mostly plants. Her brain was about as big as a chimpanzee's, about one-third of the volume of a modern human's.

The remains of more than 300 *A. afarensis* individuals have been found, making it one of the best-known fossil hominids. Having the remains of so many individuals has revealed that there were noticeable physical difference between the sexes, with males half as large again as females, weighing 93 pounds (42 kg) compared to a female's 64 pounds (29 kg).

About 40 percent of Lucy's skeleton was found. She was probably around twelve when she died, making her a young adult. For her species, forty would have been a good age.

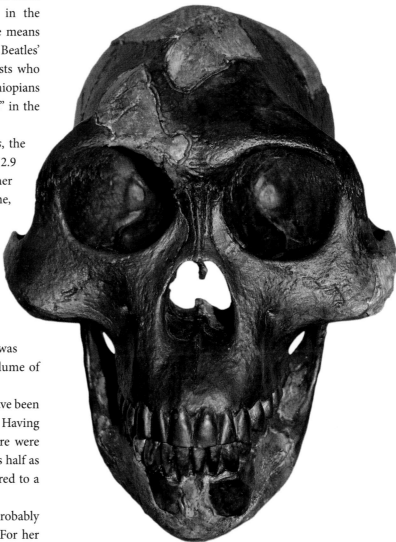

OPPOSITE: Lucy's skeleton has shown that she walked upright on two legs.

ABOVE: With strong jaws, Lucy probably ate mostly plants.

Australopithecus africanus

PERIOD: Neogene
EPOCH: Pliocene
DISTRIBUTION: South Africa
SIZE: Males 4 ft. 6 in. (1.38 m), females 3 ft. 9 in. (1.15 m)

The discovery of *Australopithecus africanus* in 1924 confirmed that Africa was the cradle of humanity. The species was first described from a fossil skull called the "Taung child," named after the small town in northern South Africa where it was found.

A. africanus was similar to *A. afarensis*, which lived earlier but was discovered later. It was similar in size, with long arms and hands adapted for climbing and a sloping face. Males were substantially bigger than females at 4 feet 6 inches (1.38 m) compared to 3 feet 9 inches (1.15 m) and weighing 90 pounds (41 kg) compared to 66 pounds (30 kg). However, its skeleton has revealed that it was better at walking upright than *A. afarensis* and had a slightly larger brain. Its hands have also shown that it could grip strongly between finger and thumb.

By using chemical analysis of teeth to reveal what *A. africanus* ate and where their food came from, scientists have concluded that females roamed more widely than males. This may be because females left their childhood homes when they reached adulthood to move into other groups; chimpanzees do the same.

The Taung child lived 2.8 million years ago. He or she was just over three years old with a full set of milk teeth. The skull, which has puncture marks at the base of the eye sockets, was found amid fragments of eggshells and the bones of small animals such as rodents and lizards. This suggests that the child was killed by an eagle, which would have made the holes in the skull with its beak and talons and discarded the bones in the detritus of its nest.

OPPOSITE: A sculptor works on reconstructing the head of *A. africanus*.

ABOVE: Damage to the Taung child's skull has suggested it was killed by an eagle.

PERIOD: Quaternary
EPOCH: Pleistocene
DISTRIBUTION: East Africa
SIZE: 3 ft. 3 in.–4 ft. 6 in. (1–1.35 m)

Homo habilis

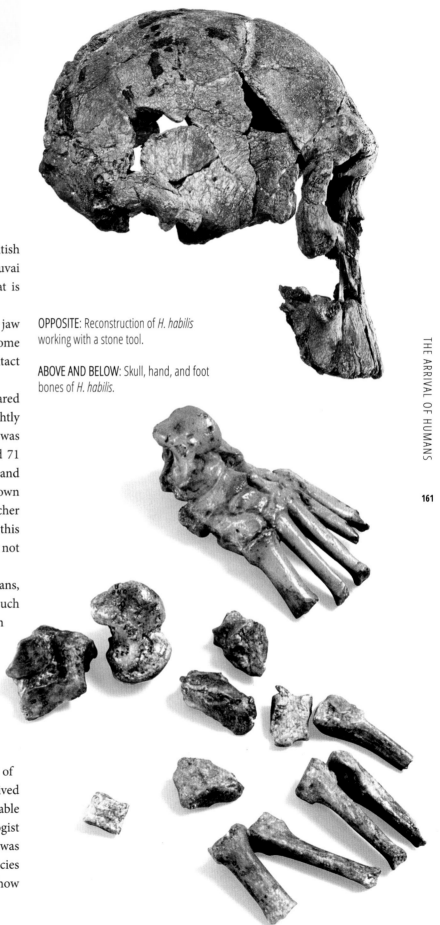

*H*omo habilis was discovered in the early 1960s by British anthropologists Mary and Louis Leakey in the Olduvai Gorge in Tanzania, a site in Africa's Rift Valley that is legendary for its fossil humans.

In 1960 their team found the top of a skull and the lower jaw of a child, as well as some wrist and hand bones, along with some foot bones from an adult. Three years later, they found a more intact adult skull and another one with well-preserved teeth.

Altogether, this evidence pointed to a new species. Compared with other ancient humans of the same period, it had a more lightly built skull and a larger brain, twice the size of a chimpanzee's. It was 3 feet 3 inches to 4 feet 6 inches (1–1.35 m) tall and weighed 71 pounds (32 kg). Its teeth were smaller and its hands were strong and mobile. The same rocks also contained some of the earliest known stone tools—axes and scrapers that might have been used to butcher and skin animals. The Leakeys and their colleagues decided that this species was a toolmaker and could be categorized as a human, not an ape. They named it *Homo habilis*—"handy man."

H. habilis seemed to fill a gap between more apelike humans, such as Lucy and the Taung child, and more modern species, such as *Homo erectus* (see pages 166–67) which at that time had been found only in Asia. Was this the point at which humans moved from the woods to the plains and developed the traits we most associate with them, such as tool use and hunting?

We still don't know, and *H. habilis* remains one of the most mysterious members of the human family. Some scientists have argued that it belongs with the genus *Australopithecus* instead of *Homo*. This is because *H. habilis* had, for example, relatively long apelike arms. And discoveries of *H. erectus* in Africa have also revealed that this species lived alongside *H. habilis* for half a million years, making it less probable that *H. habilis* was the ancestor of *H. erectus*. In 2014 anthropologist Bernard Wood, who has studied *H. habilis* almost since it was discovered, wrote in the scientific journal *Nature* that the species "should remind us of how much we don't know, rather than how much we do."

OPPOSITE: Reconstruction of *H. habilis* working with a stone tool.

ABOVE AND BELOW: Skull, hand, and foot bones of *H. habilis*.

Paranthropus boisei

PERIOD: Quaternary
EPOCH: Pleistocene
DISTRIBUTION: Eastern Africa
SIZE: Males 4 ft. 6 in. (1.37 m), females 4 ft. (1.24 m)

*P*aranthropus boisei was made to chew, having massive back teeth four times the size of a modern human's. These were powered by jaw muscles so large that the skull had a crest for them to attach to.

No wonder the species has been nicknamed "Nutcracker Man." In fact, chemical studies of its teeth show that it ate mostly grasses—an unusual diet for an early human. With such low-quality food, *P. boisei* would have needed to eat large amounts, hence the need for strong teeth and jaws. This apparatus gave the species a broad, dish-shaped face.

P. boisei was discovered in 1959 by British anthropologist Mary Leakey in the Olduvai Gorge in Tanzania. Since then further fossils have been found in Ethiopia, Kenya, and Malawi, dating from 2.3 million to 1.2 million years ago. It was 4 feet to 4 feet 6 inches (1.24–1.37 m) tall and weighed 75 to 108 pounds (34–49 kg). It was one of the first ancient humans to leave the forests and spend more time on the plains.

Two other species of fossil human with similarly strong teeth and jaws have been discovered: *P. robustus*, which lived in East Africa 2.5 million years ago, and *P. aethiopicus*, which lived in South Africa at the same time as *P. boisei*. Based on their heavily built skulls, they are known as the "robust" australopithecines. They are seen as a side group of the human family, closely related to each other but not direct ancestors of later species in the human lineage. In all, they lived for about 1.5 million years and disappeared from the fossil record about 1 million years ago.

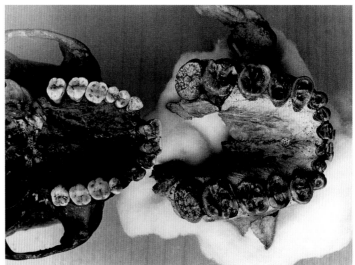

ABOVE LEFT: Louis and Mary Leakey working in the Olduvai Gorge, Kenya.

ABOVE RIGHT: *P. boisei* (right) had much bigger teeth than modern humans (left).

OPPOSITE: *P. boisei* is nicknamed "Nutcracker Man" for its large jaw.

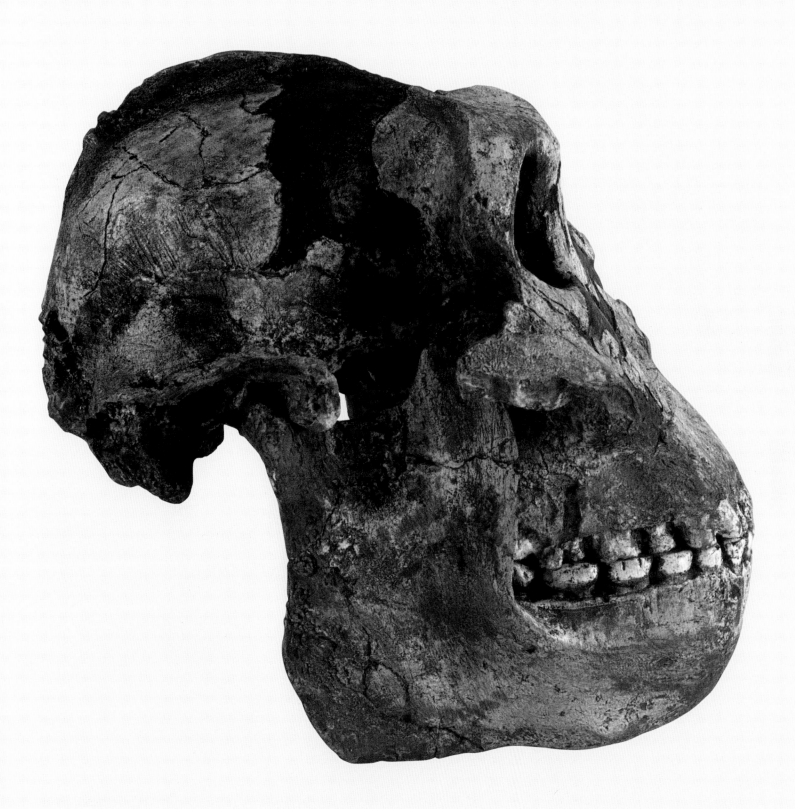

Australopithecus sediba

PERIOD: Quaternary
EPOCH: Pleistocene
DISTRIBUTION: South Africa
SIZE: 4 ft. (1.27 m)

One of the great mysteries of the human story is how our ancestors evolved from more apelike forms into something that looks more like us—attributes that scientists would class as belonging to the group *Homo*. *Australopithecus sediba* might offer a clue to that change. It lived just under 2 million years ago, around the same time as *Homo habilis* and *Homo erectus*. This might mean it was an ancestor of either or both of those species, or it might mean that it belongs in a different, parallel branch of the human family tree.

A. sediba is a recent discovery. The first specimen, a fossil collarbone, was found in 2008 by the nine-year-old son of South African paleoanthropologist Lee Berger. The bone came from inside the Malapa Cave, in an area of northwest South Africa dubbed the "Cradle of Humankind" after the many fossil humans found there.

Excavations revealed skeletons belonging to an adult male and female, a young male around the age of twelve, and three young children. All were found at the bottom of the cave; it is possible they had entered, perhaps seeking water, and fallen to their deaths. The young male's arm bones were broken as if he had fallen headfirst from a great height.

The skeleton of *A. sediba* shows a mixture of features that are found in older and younger species. Like other australopithecines, it has a small brain and long arms. However, its skeleton was better adapted for upright walking than earlier species.

Aspects of its teeth and face were also closer to modern humans, and its hands would have been capable of powerful gripping and precise movements. Together, its arms, legs, and hands were those of an animal that was adapted for life both in the trees and on the ground, and perhaps capable of using tools.

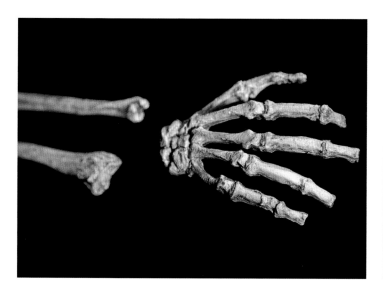

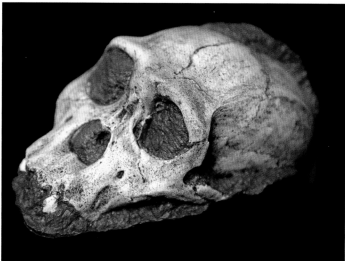

OPPOSITE: *A. sediba* mixed features found in older and younger species.

ABOVE: *A. sediba* had strong hands and might have used tools.

ABOVE RIGHT: Skull of *A. sediba* from the Malapa Cave.

PERIOD: Quaternary
EPOCH: Pleistocene
DISTRIBUTION: Africa, Asia
SIZE: 4 ft. 9 in.–6 ft. (1.45–1.85 m)

Homo erectus

In 1891 the Dutch anatomist Eugène Dubois was searching Indonesia for evidence of the missing evolutionary link between humans and apes. Digging at Trinil, on the banks of the Solo River on Java, his team found the top of a skull and a tooth. The next year they found a thighbone at the same site.

The thighbone was so similar to a modern human's that Dubois concluded it must have come from a creature that walked on two legs. He called the discovery *Pithecanthropus erectus*, the "upright apeman," and estimated it at about 1 million years old. Dubbed "Java Man," it caused a public sensation.

This species is now known as *Homo erectus*, the "upright human," because we have realized that instead of belonging with the apes it is closer to *Homo sapiens*. Indeed, it is the oldest species that's generally accepted as one of our ancestors.

H. erectus was the largest human up to that point—Lucy would have come up to only its waist. It was 4 feet 9 inches to 6 feet (1.45–1.85 m) tall and weighed 88 to 150 pounds (40–68 kg). It would have had no problem walking long distances, and its brain was nearly as big as that of *H. sapiens*.

H. erectus lived in a huge range of environments and climates from South Africa to China. It made the most sophisticated tools up to that date, including the first stone axes. Marks on animal bones have revealed that these tools were used for butchery, making *H. erectus* the first human to eat significant amounts of meat. Evidence of controlled burning at sites in South Africa and Israel have led some scientists to believe that it used fire to cook its food.

H. erectus survived for 2 million years—longer than any other human. Java was not its first home—that was Africa, where the species is sometimes called *H. ergaster*—but it was its last stronghold. In 2020 an international team revealed the latest known specimens, also from alongside the Solo River, dating from as recently as 108,000 years ago.

Dubois's work continues to yield new discoveries. In 2014 Josephine Joordens, an archaeologist at the University of Leiden in Holland, noticed a zigzag pattern carved in a freshwater mussel shell collected by Dubois. The shell was 500,000 years old, making the zigzag the oldest known abstract pattern—perhaps art—made by any human.

ABOVE: A 1.5-million-year-old *H. erectus* footprint in Kenya.

OPPOSITE: *H. erectus* survived longer than any other human species so far.

Megalochelys atlas

PERIOD: Neogene–Quaternary
EPOCH: Pliocene–Pleistocene
DISTRIBUTION: Asia
SIZE: 8 ft. (2.5 m) long

Megalochelys atlas, the Siwaliks giant tortoise, was the largest land-dwelling tortoise to have lived. It was at least twenty times heavier than the giant tortoises of the Galápagos, weighing 2,200 to 4,400 pounds (1,000–2,000 kg), and the top of its shell would have reached as high as a human. By stretching its neck, it would have been able to reach several yards up into the trees to browse. Its remains are known from northern India down to Thailand and Myanmar, and they date from about 5 to 2 million years ago.

The largest tortoises today are found on the islands of the Galápagos and the Seychelles—sites that humans have reached only in the past few hundred years. Once, however, there were dozens of species of giant tortoise living all across the world.

A tortoise's shell is no match for humans armed with stone tools. Tortoises are easy to find, catch, and transport, and they can survive for long periods without food and water—they have been described as the earliest form of canned food.

About 100 species of tortoise, small and large, have become extinct in the past 2 million years. The timings of human arrival and giant tortoise extinction are closely matched across Asia—meaning that the Siwaliks giant tortoise may have been one of the first species driven to extinction by human hunting.

168

RIGHT: *Megalochelys* may have been one of the first species driven extinct by humans.

PERIOD: Quaternary
EPOCH: Pleistocene
DISTRIBUTION: Africa, Europe
SIZE: Males 5 ft. 9 in. (1.75 m), females 5 ft. (1.57 m)

Homo heidelbergensis

*H*omo heidelbergensis* was named after remains found in a quarry near Heidelberg, Germany, in 1907. Only a jawbone was found, since dated at 600,000 years old. The bone was large and heavy, similar to the jaw of *Homo erectus*, but it had small teeth like a modern human. Anthropologist Otto Schoetensack identified it as a new species.

This made *H. heidelbergensis* the first human to live in Europe. Its bones have since been found across the continent, from the Petralona Cave in northeast Greece to Boxgrove in Sussex, England—making it the first human to reach the British Isles.

H. heidelbergensis was strongly built and similar to *H. sapiens* in body and brain size. European populations were broad as well as tall, well built for cold winters. Males were 5 feet 9 inches (1.75 m) tall and females 5 feet (1.57 m) tall, weighing 136 pounds (62 kg) and 112 pounds (51 kg) respectively. It lived from 800,000 to 200,000 years ago.

It has also been found in eastern and southern Africa, and it may have reached India and China. The African populations are thought to be the ancestors of *H. sapiens*, while European groups are probably the ancestors of the Neanderthals.

H. heidelbergensis had more sophisticated technology than any human up to that point. Hundreds of powerful and well-made stone axes have been found at Boxgrove, while 400,000-year-old spears with wooden shafts and stone tips have been found at Schöningen, Germany.

The Schöningen site also contains the butchered remains of horses, making it the earliest record of humans hunting big game with spears. A site of a similar age at Terra Amata, near Nice in southern France, held remains of simple wooden shelters that are among the oldest evidence of humans living in constructions they had built themselves.

ABOVE: A 450,000-year-old thighbone of *H. heidelbergensis* excavated in France.

BELOW: *H. heidelbergensis* was identified from this jawbone found in Germany in 1907.

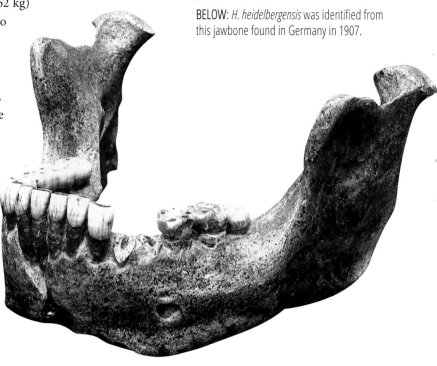

PERIOD: Quaternary
EPOCH: Pleistocene
DISTRIBUTION: Australia
SIZE: 10 ft. (3 m) long, 6 ft. 6 in. (2 m) tall

Diprotodon

The bunyip is the most fearsome monster in Aboriginal Australian mythology. It lurks in swamps, lakes, and rivers, and it drags anyone who strays too close to their doom.

The giant wombat *Diprotodon optatum* is one of the animals that might have inspired stories of the bunyip, through some combination of memories passed down the millennia and stories spun around its bones. It would not have preyed on humans; it was an herbivore. However, as the largest known marsupial, it was still a spectacular animal, standing 10 feet (3 m) long and 6 feet 6 inches (2 m) tall, and weighing 6,170 pounds (2,800 kg).

Remains of *Diprotodon* have been found across Australia. Analysis of the growth patterns and chemical makeup of its teeth has shown that these animals were migratory, traveling hundreds of miles to find food and water in the same way as do African herbivores such as wildebeests and elephants. They were the only known migratory marsupial. Another similarity between *Diprotodon* and large African animals revealed by the fossils is that the females and young lived in family groups separate from males, who probably fought each other for mates and dominance.

Diprotodon disappeared around 46,000 years ago, during a time of hotter climate and drought. It was also 10,000 years after the first humans reached Australia. The most complete *Diprotodon* skeleton has a hole shaped like the point of a spear in its ribs. Whatever the balance of causes, a wave of extinction wiped out every mammal, bird, and reptile on the continent that weighed more than 220 pounds (100 kg). Other casualties included 6-foot 6-inch (2-m)-tall kangaroos and marsupial lions.

As well as hunting large animals, humans may have contributed to their extinction by changing the landscape. Aboriginal societies, for example, have used controlled wildfires to improve conditions for food plants and game animals.

171

LEFT: The giant wombat *Diprotodon* was the largest marsupial in evolutionary history.

Homo floresiensis

PERIOD: Quaternary
EPOCH: Pleistocene
DISTRIBUTION: Indonesia
SIZE: 3 ft. 3 in. (1 m) tall

The 2004 announcement of *Homo floresiensis*, otherwise known as "the hobbit," caused a stir. A new species of human, only 3 feet 3 inches (1 m) tall and weighing 62 pounds (28 kg), that lived in Asia at the same time as modern humans was a sensational discovery. So sensational, in fact, that some scientists argued that the bones discovered in Liang Bua limestone cave on the Indonesian island of Flores must have belonged to a group of *Homo sapiens* suffering from some form of dwarfing condition.

That idea was put to rest by the 2016 announcement of 700,000-year-old bones from another site on Flores called Mata Menge. Whatever *H. floresiensis* was, it was around for a long time— the original skeletons from Liang Bua are only 60,000 years old.

That leaves two theories for the origin of the hobbit. One is that it was descended from a group of *Homo erectus* that had arrived on Flores a million years ago—the age of the oldest stone tools found on the island—and evolved a much smaller body size. The other is that the hobbits were descended from an older, smaller, ancient human, such as *Homo habilis*, that had migrated out of Africa and settled in Asia.

Islands are home to many dwarf animal species. There is little threat from predators, and food and space are limited, which leads large species to evolve smaller bodies. For example, remains of dwarf elephants only 3 feet 3 inches (1 m) tall have been found on many islands, including Flores in Southeast Asia and Sicily, Cyprus, and Crete in the Mediterranean. A small, island-dwelling human would fit this pattern, but if *H. erectus* became *H. floresiensis* in a few hundred thousand years, it was a more drastic change than any other in human evolution.

One thing in favor of *H. erectus* is that it was in the right place at the right time to evolve into the hobbit. No other older human has been found outside Africa; if another species traveled across Asia and settled on Flores, we have no evidence of its journey.

The debate was upended again in 2019 with the discovery of another species of small human from a southeast Asian island. This was *Homo luzonensis*, described from a mix of teeth, hand and foot bones, and thighbones found in Callao Cave on Luzon in the Philippines.

The teeth of *H. luzonensis* were similar to those of more recent human species, indicating perhaps that humans, like elephants, have shrunk more than once while living on islands. But the hands and feet were more like those of far older humans, such as australopithecines, supporting the idea that they were descended from a more ancient ancestor. Establishing where—and whom— these diminutive humans came from awaits further discoveries.

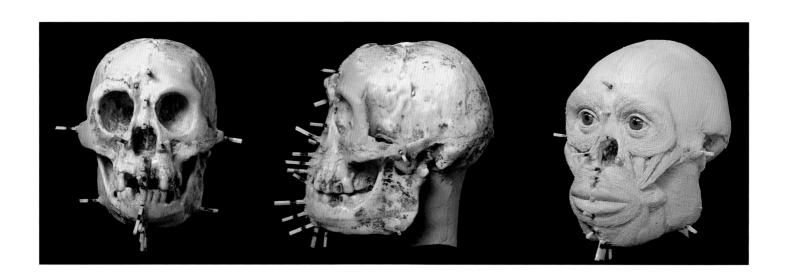

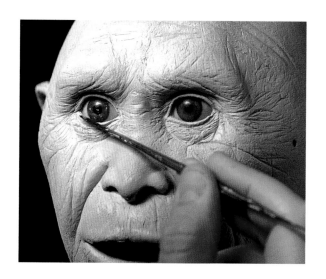

FAR LEFT: From skull to face—reconstructing the hobbit's appearance.

ABOVE: Liang Bua cave, where the "hobbit" was discovered.

LEFT: Skull of *H. floresiensis*.

Arctodus simus

PERIOD: Quaternary
EPOCH: Pleistocene
DISTRIBUTION: North America
SIZE: About 5 ft. (1.5 m) tall

The short-faced bear *Arctodus simus* was the largest carnivorous mammal to have lived in North America. The largest males may have topped 2,200 pounds (1,000 kg)—twice the weight of a polar bear—and would have stood more than 10 feet (3 m) tall on their hind legs.

This bear is known from more than 100 sites across North America from Alaska to Mexico. DNA recovered from ancient bones has shown that its closest living relative is the spectacled bear, which lives in the Andes of South America.

Ideas about the bear's diet and behavior vary, but it probably lived much like the black and grizzly bears that inhabit North America today. Wear on the teeth of some short-faced bear specimens has pointed to an omnivorous diet that included a lot of plant material, while chemical analysis of other bones has suggested a meat-based diet. Modern bears' diet varies from place to place, depending on what food is available, and *Arctodus* may have been the same.

Any meat in the bear's diet was probably scavenged instead of hunted. They were big enough to chase other carnivores, such as saber-toothed cats and dire wolves, away from their kills, but they would not have been fast enough to catch large animals such as deer.

Short-faced bears appeared about 2 million years ago and survived until about 11,000 years ago, disappearing soon after the end of the last ice age, along with many other large North American mammals, including giant beavers and ground sloths.

The Pleistocene was a time of rapid climate change. It was also a few thousand years after humans crossed from Siberia into North America across a land bridge exposed by falling sea levels. Humans may therefore have been a possible factor in the bears' extinction. We don't know if prehistoric Americans hunted *Arctodus*, although their Native American descendants are known to have hunted bears for food and fur.

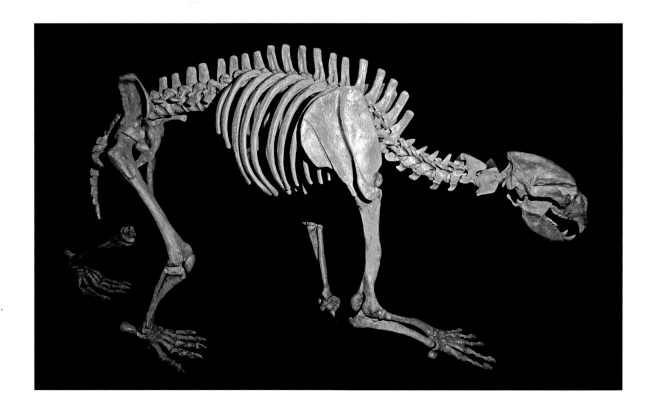

RIGHT: The bear *Arctodus* was North America's largest carnivorous mammal.

OPPOSITE: *Arctodus* ranged across North America during the last ice age.

Glyptodon

PERIOD: Quaternary
EPOCH: Pleistocene
DISTRIBUTION: South America
SIZE: 10 ft. (3 m) long, 5 ft. (1.5 m) tall

There are several ways to avoid being eaten. You can run, and you can hide. But one look at *Glyptodon* reveals that it was neither swift nor inconspicuous. Instead—like tortoises, some dinosaurs before it, and its relatives the armadillos—it opted for armor.

Two million years ago, *Glyptodon* would have been hard to miss as it browsed on the plains of South America. It was the size and shape of a Volkswagen Beetle: 10 feet (3 m) long, 5 feet (1.5 m) high, and weighing up to 2 tons. A sizable chunk of its weight was in its shell, which was made up of more than 1,000 bony plates, each 1 inch (2.5 cm) thick.

One of the few creatures capable of damaging that shell was another *Glyptodon*. The animal wielded a 3-foot 3-inch (1-m)-long tail like a massive spiked club. Scientists have suggested, judging from the evidence of fractures in fossil shells, that it was used mainly as a weapon in fights between males.

Glyptodon was one of the last of a large group of armored armadillos that evolved in South America when the continent was separate from North America. Three million years ago that changed, when plate tectonics and volcanic activity created a land bridge between the two continents.

Species traveled across this bridge in both directions. Generally, those from the north won out, but *Glyptodon* was one of the southerners that survived, making it as far north as what is now the southern United States.

Glyptodon's armor seems to have offered protection against all hunters except humans. Like many other large American mammals, *Glyptodon* disappeared 11,000 years ago, the same time that humans arrived in the Americas. There's some evidence that the first Americans used its shell as a shelter.

OPPOSITE: The giant *Glyptodon* is related to modern armadillos.

RIGHT: Prehistoric humans might have made shelters from *Glyptodon*'s shell.

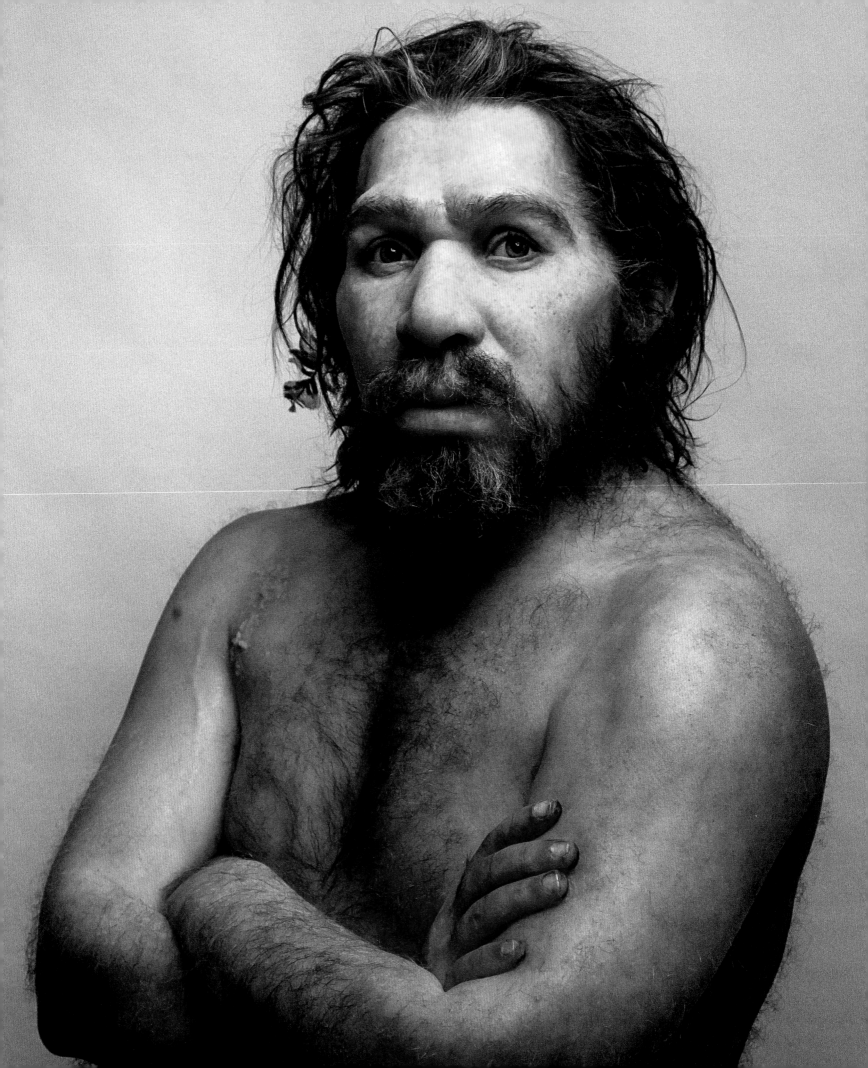

Neanderthal

CLASSIFICATION: *Homo neanderthalensis*
PERIOD: Quaternary
EPOCH: Pleistocene
DISTRIBUTION: Europe, Asia
SIZE: Males 5 ft 6 in. (1.64 m), females 5 ft. (1.55 m)

Neanderthals were named from bones found in the Neander Valley in Germany in 1856. They were the first species of humans besides our own to be discovered, and possibly the last to live alongside us.

For the best part of 100 years, Neanderthals have been caricatured as the classic grunting, club-waving cave dwellers. Now we know that while they may have looked different to us, with broad faces, barrel chests, and relatively short limbs well adapted for cold weather (and larger brains than *Homo sapiens*), little separated Neanderthal technology and culture from *H. sapiens* of the same time.

Neanderthals made sophisticated stone tools, including spears for hunting big game and awls for making holes in hides that were then laced together into clothes. They made tar for gluing stone tools to wooden hafts. They cared for their sick and injured and used medicinal plants. They buried their dead with care. They made symbolic, abstract patterns, and they may have played musical instruments—a hollow bear's thighbone found in Divje Babe cave in Slovenia closely resembles a flute.

Neanderthals were probably descended from *Homo heidelbergensis*, the first ancient human to reach Europe. The earliest Neanderthal remains are about 430,000 years old, from the Atapuerca Mountains in northern Spain. Fossils show they reached as far as Wales in the northwest, Syria in the south, and Uzbekistan in the east.

Since the late 1990s, our understanding of Neanderthal history has increased substantially, thanks to studies of their DNA taken from ancient bones. These results have shown that Neanderthals shared 99.7 percent of their DNA with us. They have also revealed that when modern humans and Neanderthals first encountered one another in the Middle East about 50,000 years ago, they interbred. About 1 to 2 percent of the genomes of humans living outside Africa is inherited from Neanderthals.

Modern humans started moving into Europe about 45,000 years ago. By about 40,000 years ago, Neanderthal life in Europe had disappeared. Many possible causes of this extinction have been suggested. Environmental change may have been a factor—Europe went through a spell of cold, dry climate at this time—but our species is almost certainly part of the story.

Genetic and archaeological evidence shows that Neanderthals lived in small populations that were isolated and inbred, leaving them vulnerable to change and competition. Our species and theirs lived alongside one another for thousands of years, but modern humans seem to have had some competitive edge, whether in technology, togetherness, or both, that enabled them to gradually replace the Neanderthals. They may also have carried diseases that Neanderthals were not immune to, just as later European colonists did on their journeys around the world.

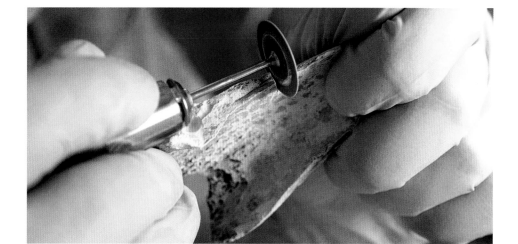

OPPOSITE: Neanderthals had sophisticated technology and culture.

RIGHT: DNA extracted from bones has revealed that Neanderthals bred with modern humans.

Woolly mammoth

CLASSIFICATION: *Mammuthus primigenius*
PERIOD: Quaternary
EPOCH: Pleistocene
DISTRIBUTION: Europe, Asia, North America
SIZE: 10 ft. (3 m) tall

The mammoth was one of the animals that first revealed the reality of extinction. In 1796 the great French anatomist Georges Cuvier presented bones and tusks found in Siberia, declaring that they showed "the existence of a world previous to ours, destroyed by some kind of catastrophe."

We now know that there were many different species of mammoths. The oldest appeared in Africa 5 million years ago, and they reached Europe 3 million years ago. The woolly mammoth (*Mammuthus primigenius*) evolved in eastern Siberia 400,000 years ago and spread across the grasslands of the Northern Hemisphere, reaching China, Spain, and the northern United States. It was about the size of an African elephant, standing 10 feet (3 m) tall and weighing 11,000 pounds (5,000 kg).

Mammoths lived alongside humans —first Neanderthals, and then *Homo sapiens*—for tens of thousands of years. Humans hunted them for their meat and made tools, art, and shelters from their tusks and bones. Prehistoric art shows how much humans valued mammoths, with their likenesses painted onto cave walls in France, Spain, and Russia, as well as being carved into ivory, bone, and stone.

The end of the last ice age about 12,000 years ago had a negative impact on the woolly mammoth population, which had not adapted for a warmer, wetter climate and the changes to plant life that resulted. By 10,000 years ago, the mammoths were reduced to small, isolated groups in Siberia and Alaska, unable to reproduce quickly enough to repair the toll taken by hunting. The last known mammoths lived in Arctic Siberia 4,000 years ago, during the time when ancient Egyptians were building the great pyramids.

Well-preserved mammoth corpses have been discovered frozen in the tundra for hundreds of years. DNA was first extracted from such remains in 1994, and a genome sequence was published in 2008.

Now there are dreams of re-creating the mammoth. A team at Harvard University led by the geneticist George Church is working to reprogram elephant cells with mammoth genes for cold-weather adaptations such as thick hair and body fat. They hope to produce embryos and living young that will be raised by elephants in zoos before eventually being released to roam Siberia once again.

LEFT: Woolly mammoths lived across the northern hemisphere until a few millennia ago.

Jos: Dinkel del et lith.

1

2

Printed by Hullmandel & Walton.

6
THE LAST MILLENNIUM

OPPOSITE: A nineteenth-century drawing of a dodo made from a museum specimen.

PERIOD

QUATERNARY

EPOCH

END OF HOLOCENE–START OF ANTHROPOCENE

Throughout Earth's history, species have always come and gone. At present, however, the United Nations Environment Programme estimates that up to 150 species are becoming extinct *every day*. Even if the true figure was one-hundredth of this, animals and plants are still disappearing thousands of times faster than at most times in history. Many scientists believe that we are already in the middle of a mass extinction.

It has become common to label this period the Anthropocene—the age of humans. This is not yet an official time period in the same way as the Jurassic, for example, but what's not in doubt is that humans have already had a massive impact on the planet.

In total, about a million species are currently under threat of extinction. This includes one-third of amphibians, one-quarter of mammals, one-fifth of reptiles, one in eight bird species, and one in twenty fish. We know little about our impact on insects and other invertebrates, and the sea remains a mystery—more people have been to the moon than to the deepest parts of the ocean.

LEFT: A green turtle swims over damaged coral in Hawaii.

OPPOSITE: The Huia, a Hawaiian bird, became extinct around 1907.

Extinction is not only a tragedy for the species that die out—many of them are disappearing before we have been able to learn about them. Wild insects pollinate our crops. Worms, insects, fungi, microscopic life, and hordes of other species keep the soil, water, and air healthy. Most medicines have been first found in wild plants, and rain forests and coral reefs could harbor life-saving medicines waiting to be discovered. As we destroy nature, we undermine ourselves.

The major threats to wild animals are loss of their habitat, pollution, invasive species, hunting, and trade. Climate change is already bringing vast wildfires, melting ice, and damaging coral reefs. It will change the environment for every species. Not all will be able to adapt.

Large animals such as rhinoceroses, apes, and big cats are most at risk. They are the first to be targeted by hunters. They breed more slowly and have fewer offspring, so their numbers take longer to increase.

Animals on islands are also especially vulnerable. Many have not encountered predators or diseases for millions of years, meaning they have lost defenses against them. When humans arrive, bringing rats, cats, pigs, and dogs—along with their infections—it often spells doom. Remote islands such as Madagascar, Hawaii, and New Zealand have lost many of their species in the past few centuries.

The news is not all grim. Around the world, skilled and dedicated conservationists are striving to save species by preserving their habitats or through captive breeding programs. Some are even trying to resurrect extinct species through genetic engineering and cloning. However, high-tech, expensive approaches can save only a handful of species. If we want to protect wildlife, we need to protect wild places.

Sometimes the good news is a surprise. Naturalists regularly find species they thought had become extinct hundreds or even millions of years ago; these have become known as Lazarus species, after the man Jesus is said to have brought back from the dead. These discoveries are a cause for joy but also a reminder of how little we know. The challenge now is to understand and protect as many as we can of the millions of other species in the only place in the universe known to harbor life.

LEFT: Beavers have recently been reintroduced in the wild in southern England.

OPPOSITE: One of the last two northern white rhinoceroses grazes in a secure paddock in Kenya.

Baby panda in
China, one of several
hundred born in
captivity each year.

Elephant birds

STATUS: Extinct about 1000 CE
DISTRIBUTION: Madagascar
SIZE: 5–10 ft. (1.5–3 m) tall

When Europeans first arrived in Madagascar in the 1600s, they heard stories of large flightless birds living in remote parts of the island. These tales were almost certainly passed down instead of experienced firsthand, because the evidence points to Madagascar's elephant birds becoming extinct about 1,000 years ago. Even so, the birds' bones were easy to find, and the remains of its eggs—the largest of any animal—were used as bowls into the nineteenth century.

There were four species of elephant birds. The smallest was about 5 feet (1.5 m) tall, while the largest, *Vorombe titan*, was 10 feet (3 m) tall and averaged 143 pounds (650 kg). That makes it the biggest bird to have lived—as tall as an African elephant and as heavy as a cow. The moas of New Zealand, a group of giant birds that became extinct around 1300, were about the same height but much lighter.

Elephant birds were probably forest-dwelling herbivores. Ancient DNA taken from remains has revealed that their closest living relative is the kiwi from New Zealand, more than 7,000 miles (11,000 km) away. This means that the ancestors of elephant birds flew to Madagascar and evolved to be huge and flightless later.

Madagascar's isolation from the rest of Africa has left it with many animals, such as lemurs, found nowhere else. But it has also lost many species, hunted to extinction by humans. As well as elephant birds, these include giant lemurs that weighed as much as a human and several species of hippopotamus. Their disappearance has changed Madagascar's ecosystems and endangered other species such as the plants that relied on elephant birds to spread their seeds.

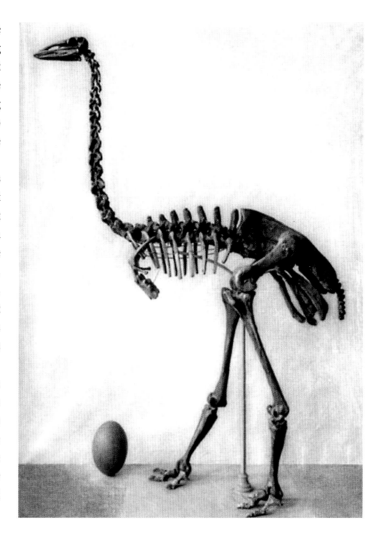

OPPOSITE: The largest elephant birds weighed as much as a cow.

RIGHT: *Aepyornis maximus,* one of four species of elephant birds.

Aurochs

CLASSIFICATION: *Bos primigenius*
STATUS: Extinct 1627
DISTRIBUTION: Europe, Asia, North Africa
SIZE: 5 ft. 3 in. (1.6 m) tall, 2,200 pounds (1,000 kg)

No wild aurochs has lived for centuries. But as the ancestors of domestic cattle, the aurochs can lay claim to a billion descendants living worldwide. The species is gone, but its genes survive.

Once aurochs lived across Europe, Asia, and North Africa. In prehistoric times, they were one of Europe's largest animals, bigger than a bison, and bearing magnificent horns. They are recorded in the famous cave paintings at Lascaux and Chauvet in France. They are the wild cattle depicted in ancient Greek and Babylonian art, and they are mentioned in the Bible and the writings of Julius Caesar.

But even thousands of years ago, hunting was killing aurochs faster than they could breed, while the spread of farming pushed them off the land. By the thirteenth century, they were confined to the forests of Eastern Europe. The last recorded animals died in Poland in 1627.

Aurochs were first domesticated about 10,000 years ago in the Middle East. These animals were the ancestors of European cattle. A second population in Asia became the zebu, the humped cow of India.

The first attempt to re-create the aurochs by selectively breeding domestic cows occurred in the 1930s. Today, armed with genetic information taken from living cows and aurochs' bones, conservationists aim to fine-tune this process. They are focusing on the oldest breeds and those whose DNA shows they are most similar to their wild ancestors, such as the Spanish Sayaguesa.

As well as bringing back wild cattle, these "rewilding" projects aim to restore the environmental role they played. Large herbivores shape the landscape by spreading seeds and trampling and eating plants. Returning an aurochs-like animal to Europe, some hope, would help to restore its ecosystems and wild places.

LEFT: A woodcut of an aurochs made in 1560.

OPPOSITE: Aurochs were one of Europe's largest mammals.

FOLLOWING PAGES: Cave art in Lascaux, France, shows aurochs, deer, and horses.

Dodo

CLASSIFICATION: *Raphus cucullatus*
STATUS: Extinct about 1700
DISTRIBUTION: Mauritius
SIZE: 3 ft. 3 in. (1 m) tall, 33 lb. (15 kg)

The island of Mauritius was thrown up by undersea volcanoes about 7 million years ago. Sometime after that, a species of pigeon arrived from Southeast Asia. There were no predators on Mauritius, so natural selection made the pigeon large, and it lost the ability to fly, nesting on the ground and eating fruit that fell from trees.

In 1505 Portuguese sailors landed on Mauritius. The earliest drawings show a slim bird, not the fat caricature of later portraits. Late in the same century, Dutch visitors called it the *Walghvoghel*, meaning "tasteless bird," but that did not stop them from eating it. An English traveler first used the name "dodo" in 1632. The name might come from the Dutch words for lazy (*dodoor*) or fat bottom (*dodaars*), or from the Portuguese word for foolish (*doudo*); or the dodo may have been named after the sound of its call.

Visitors and settlers brought rats, cats, pigs, and monkeys that ate the dodo's eggs and chicks. By the mid-1600s, many years would pass between reported sightings, with the last one being in 1688. The last bird probably died before 1700.

The dodo died out before people realized that animals could become extinct, and many eighteenth-century naturalists doubted that the bird had ever existed. The truth of its life and death emerged only in the nineteenth century, when biologists pieced together specimens scattered around European museums.

Modern studies have shown that the dodo was not a stupid, clumsy creature predestined for extinction, but an animal well adapted to its environment. It's worth remembering that it survived on Mauritius for millions of years—considerably longer than our species has so far managed.

OPPOSITE: The dodo was not as fat and clumsy as it is often portrayed.

RIGHT: A portrait of the dodo by the Dutch artist Roelant Savery.

Steller's sea cow

CLASSIFICATION: *Hydrodamalis gigas*
STATUS: Extinct 1768
DISTRIBUTION: North Pacific
SIZE: 26 ft. 3 in. (8 m) long, 10 tons

Steller's sea cow saved the life of the man who gave it his name. In 1741 the German naturalist Georg Steller was part of a Russian expedition to Alaska that was shipwrecked on what is now Bering Island. The expedition's leader, Vitus Bering, died of scurvy, but Steller and half the crew survived by eating the meat of a large sea cow. By 1768—only twenty-seven years later—it was extinct, making it the first marine mammal driven to extinction by humans.

Seller's sea cow was the largest member of a group that includes the manatee and dugong. It was huge; the largest could reach 33 feet (10 m) long, bigger than an orca. It was also slow, docile, and gregarious. These characteristics made it easy meat for the hunters who traveled to Alaska to kill sea otters for their fur.

Besides attracting hunters to Alaska, the trade in otter fur may have hastened the sea cow's demise in another way. Otters eat sea urchins, which eat kelp; when large numbers of otters were killed, the urchin population boomed, causing a collapse in the kelp forests that the sea cows relied on for food.

The disappearance of Steller's sea cow helped to convince European naturalists that animals could become extinct. But the species was in trouble long before Europeans discovered it. Bones and fossils show that it once lived across the North Pacific from Japan to Mexico. The animals found by Steller and his shipmates were probably the last survivors of a much larger population that had been driven nearly to extinction as a result of hunting by indigenous peoples.

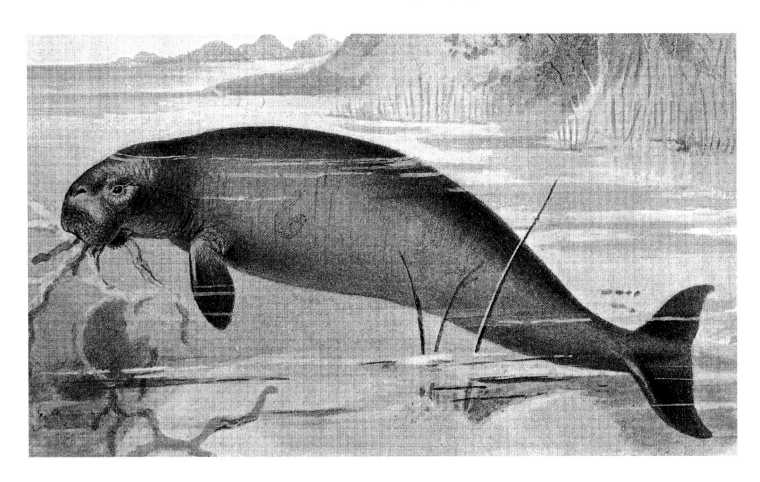

OPPOSITE: Steller's sea cow was related to dugongs and manatees.

ABOVE: Skull of Steller's sea cow. As an herbivore, it had no teeth.

BELOW: Engraving of the skeleton of Steller's sea cow.

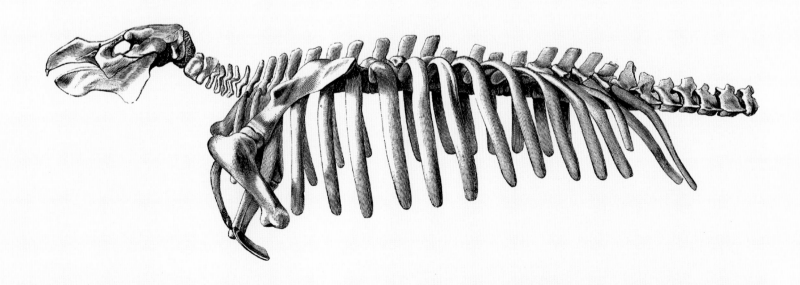

CLASSIFICATION: *Thylacinus cynocephalus*
STATUS: Extinct 1936
DISTRIBUTION: Australia
SIZE: 3 ft. 3 in. (1 m) long, 55 lb. (25 kg)

Thylacine

Thylacines lived in Australia for more than 20 million years. They were one of the few large marsupials, and the only predator, to survive past the arrival of humans in Australia about 50,000 years ago. Aboriginal Australians carved the animal's image into rocks in northwest Australia 3,000 years ago.

Thylacines died out on the mainland in the mid-1800s, perhaps because of competition with the dingoes introduced by humans. However, they survived on the island of Tasmania, 150 miles (240 km) off Australia's south coast. Thylacines were sometimes called Tasmanian tigers, because of their stripes, or Tasmanian wolves, because of their body shape.

In the 1800s, Tasmania became sheep-farming country, and thylacines were blamed for killing livestock. A bounty was offered for dead animals, and collecting for museums and zoos reduced the wild population still further. Diseases caught from introduced animals may have also taken their toll.

The last wild thylacine was shot in 1930. The only remaining animal outside Australia died in London Zoo in 1931. Finally, the last thylacine of all died in Hobart Zoo in 1936. Film footage from 1933 shows it pacing in its cage.

The thylacine's extinction left the Tasmanian devil as the largest surviving carnivorous marsupial. They too have suffered from persecution and loss of habitat, and they are now threatened by a contagious facial cancer that spreads from animal to animal.

LEFT: A photograph of the last Thylacine, which died in captivity in 1936.

Coelacanth

CLASSIFICATION: *Latimeria chalumnae*
STATUS: Critically endangered
DISTRIBUTION: Indian Ocean
SIZE: 6 ft. 6 in. (2 m), 200 lb. (90 kg)

Before 1938 it was thought that coelacanths had been extinct for 70 million years. Then a South African trawler brought up an unidentified fish from the Indian Ocean. The fish was more than 3 feet 3 inches (1 m) long, blue, and had fleshy fins that looked almost like short legs. The captain contacted the curator at the local museum, Marjorie Courtenay-Latimer, who consulted other experts. The realization that a living coelacanth had been found made headlines around the world and was hailed as one of the most important biological discoveries of the twentieth century.

It was fifteen years before another specimen was caught, and only 309 coelacanths were recorded over the next seventy-five years, mostly from the waters of the Comoro Islands in the Indian Ocean, off the coast of East Africa. In 1997 a second species of coelacanth was discovered in Indonesian waters.

We now know that coelacanths live about 650 feet (200 m) deep, spending the day in underwater caves before emerging at night to hunt fish, squid, and octopus. They home in on their prey by sensing its electrical activity, and swallow it using double-hinged jaws; it is the only vertebrate known that can swing open both its lower and upper jaws.

Coelacanths swim and burn energy slowly, needing barely half an ounce (12 g) of food a day. And they evolve slowly; fossil coelacanths 400 million years old look much like the modern species. Their bony, limb-like fins show they are among the fishes most closely related to four-legged vertebrates.

The Red List of threatened species classes the coelacanth as critically endangered—there may be fewer than 500 left. Coelacanths are not fished deliberately—they are indigestible and give humans diarrhea—but are caught accidentally. Warming seas may also disrupt their delicate, slow-motion biology, but marine reserves may help them survive.

LEFT: Fossil coelacanths look much like their living relatives.

OPPOSITE: Living coelacanths were discovered in the Indian Ocean in 1938.

Partula

CLASSIFICATION: *Partula* spp.
STATUS: Extinct and extinct in the wild
DISTRIBUTION: French Polynesia
SIZE: ½ in. (1–2 cm); ¹/₃₂ oz (1 g)

In 1967 the government of Tahiti in the South Pacific introduced the giant African land snail (*Achatina fulica*) to the island. The snails were intended to become a source of food. Instead they became a pest, devouring crop plants and spreading to other nearby islands.

In 1977 a predatory snail was introduced, with the aim of controlling the giant snails. This was the Florida rosy wolf snail (*Euglandina rosea*). Instead of eating the invaders, however, it turned on the natives.

The Society Islands, part of French Polynesia that includes Tahiti, Moorea, Raiatea, and Bora Bora, were home to dozens of species of tree snails belonging to a group called *Partula* (named after the Roman goddess of childbirth, because—unlike most snails—they produce live young instead of laying eggs). Many species of *Partula* lived on a single island or even in a single valley. Biologists studied them to understand how new species evolve, and the islanders used their jewel-like shells to make necklaces.

In the decade following its introduction, the rosy wolf snail ravaged the *Partula* snails. Of seventy-seven species, fifty-five became extinct. When they realized what was happening, conservationists and biologists swooped in to protect the surviving snails. They managed to rescue eleven species before they became extinct in the wild and set up captive breeding programs in zoos around the world. Captivity does not guarantee their survival—in 1996 one captive species, *Partula turgida*, was wiped out by a fungal infection. But other species have been able to build up strong populations.

Efforts to reintroduce *Partula* to their native islands began in 1994, using enclosures designed to exclude the rosy wolf snail. The predator thwarted the first attempts, crossing electric fences on fallen vegetation. Later efforts have been more successful, and to date more than 10,000 *Partula* snails have been released.

RIGHT: Dozens of species of *Partula* snails were wiped out by an introduced species.

Pyrenean ibex

CLASSIFICATION: *Capra pyrenaica pyrenaica*
STATUS: Extinct 2000
DISTRIBUTION: Spain, France
SIZE: 4 ft. (1.2 m) long, 132 lb. (60 kg)

The last Pyrenean ibex died in 2000, and the last Pyrenean ibex was born in 2003. That sounds impossible. In fact, the ibex is the first extinct species to be resurrected by cloning. The attempt failed, with the baby surviving for only a few minutes. But some scientists and conservationists hope that cloning can become a way to preserve endangered species and revive extinct ones.

The Pyrenean ibex, or bucardo, was a subspecies of the Iberian ibex, a wild goat that lives in the Pyrenean mountains on the border of Spain and France. It wintered in the valleys and migrated to the high mountains in spring, with males and females living separately for much of the year. Hunting for sport drove down its numbers until only a small group remained in one of Spain's national parks. By 1989 there were no male goats left.

By 1999 there was only a single animal, a twelve-year-old called Celia. A team of Spanish and French conservationists captured her and took a sample of skin cells. The following year, a falling tree killed her. To clone Celia, the scientists took the DNA from her cells and inserted it into a domestic goat's egg cell with its own DNA removed. Fifty-seven embryos were cloned from Celia's cells in this way and implanted into female ibexes. But most cloning attempts have been unsuccessful; only seven animals became pregnant, six of these miscarried, and the one baby ibex was born with fatal lung defects, which are common in cloned animals.

Cloning has become more reliable since the attempts to clone Celia, and hope remains that it can be used for conservation.

ABOVE: Attempts to clone the Pyrenean ibex have so far been unsuccessful.

CLASSIFICATION: *Panthera pardus orientalis*
STATUS: Critically endangered
DISTRIBUTION: Russia, China
SIZE: 4 ft. (1.2 m) long, 88 lb. (40 kg)

Amur leopard

Today Amur leopards are the world's rarest big cat. They once lived across a wide area of the forests of eastern Russia, China, and Korea. They are adapted for cold weather and snow, with a larger body and thicker, paler fur than other leopards.

Throughout the twentieth century, humans destroyed the leopard's forest habitat and hunted the deer that they relied on for food. They also killed the leopards for their fur, because they were seen as a threat, and to use their body parts in traditional medicines. By 1996 the Amur leopard was classed as critically endangered, and it has remained so ever since. They now live in just one small area along the Russian-Chinese border.

Around 2000 there were as few as twenty-five Amur leopards left in the wild. Conservation efforts have helped this number to rise to about ninety, the majority of which live in protected areas. Being reduced to such low numbers wiped out most of the genetic diversity in the wild population, leaving the survivors vulnerable to disease and inherited health problems.

Another 180 Amur leopards are living in zoos worldwide. There are plans to reintroduce captive animals to the wild in a Russian reserve separate from the surviving wild population; this would be the first reintroduction program for a big cat.

The Amur leopard is one of eight subspecies of leopard that once lived across Africa, Asia, and the Middle East. All have suffered from habitat loss and hunting, and four of these subspecies are now classed as critically endangered.

LEFT: The Amur leopard survives in one small area on the border of China and Russia.

Baiji

CLASSIFICATION: *Lipotes vexillifer*
STATUS: Critically endangered or extinct
DISTRIBUTION: China
SIZE: 8 ft. 3 in. (2.5 m) long, 485 lb. (220 kg)

The baiji, or Chinese river dolphin, lived in Asia's longest river, the Yangtze in China. It was descended from marine dolphins that swam upriver millions of years ago and gradually adapted to life in fresh water. There are descriptions of the dolphin in literature and folktales more than 2,000 years old, and fishermen and boatmen saw it as the embodiment of the protective goddess of the river.

In 1950 there were believed to be 6,000 baiji left. However, as China became industrialized, fishing, pollution, dam building, and collisions with boats all took their toll. Efforts to protect the species in the wild and breed it in captivity failed, with most animals dying soon after they were captured.

By 1999 only thirteen individuals could be found. The last captive animal died in 2002, and the final sighting of a wild animal was in 2004. In 2006 conservationists searched more than 2,000 miles (3,500 km) of the Yangtze without finding a single dolphin, and the species was declared probably extinct.

There's still a faint hope that the baiji might survive. Video footage taken in 2007 purports to show some baiji, and in 2016 a team of amateur conservationists claimed to have seen it leaping out of the water. However, these sightings have not been confirmed or followed up, and it is probable that the baiji is the first dolphin to be driven to extinction by humans.

There are a handful of other freshwater dolphin and porpoise species. Most, including the Yangtze finless porpoise and the Ganges River dolphin in India, are endangered, due to the same threats that wiped out the baiji.

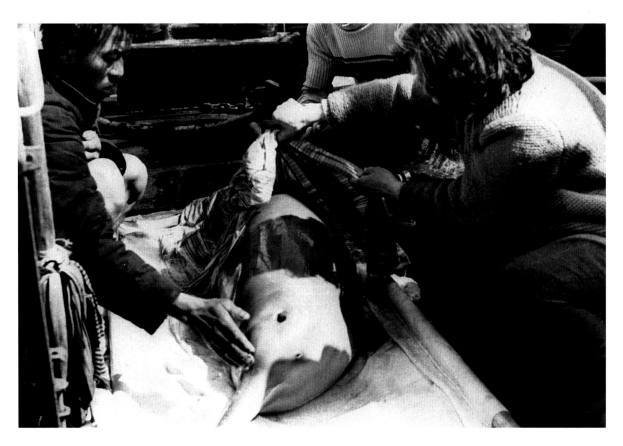

LEFT: Chinese scientists with a baiji, which lived in the Yangtze River.

Black-footed ferret

CLASSIFICATION: *Mustela nigripes*
STATUS: Endangered
DISTRIBUTION: Central North America
SIZE: 1 ft. 6 in.–2 ft. (46–61 cm) long, 2 lb. (900 g)

The black-footed ferret is one of North America's most endangered mammals and its only native ferret species. It once ranged throughout the Great Plains, but it declined during the twentieth century due to loss of its prairie habitat and to Silvatic plague, which infects both the ferret and its prairie dog prey.

When the last captive animal died in 1979, it was believed to be extinct. Then a small population was discovered when a dog on a Wyoming ranch brought in a ferret in 1981.

A captive breeding and release program organized by the US Fish and Wildlife Service aims to raise the numbers in the wild, but the population has continued to decline in the last decade. Currently about 300 ferrets live in the wild at thirty monitored sites in Wyoming, South Dakota, Montana, and Arizona.

As well as its black feet, the ferret also has black smudges around its eyes, resembling the classic "masked bandit." Its long, slender body enables it to crawl into the burrows of the prairie dog, its primary prey. Without prairie dogs, the black-footed ferret could not survive, and reestablishing the ferret requires a thriving colony of prairie dogs. However, this species has its own challenges. Over the last 100 years, more than 95 percent of historic prairie-dog range has been lost, and introduced diseases have also reduced their numbers.

RIGHT: Captive breeding has brought the black-footed ferret back from the brink.

Wallace's giant bee

CLASSIFICATION: *Megachile pluto*
STATUS: Vulnerable
DISTRIBUTION: Indonesia
SIZE: 1½ in. (4 cm) long

Although this is the world's largest bee, it has been difficult to find. In 1858 it was discovered by, and named after, Alfred Russel Wallace, the great British biologist and codiscoverer of the theory of evolution with Charles Darwin.

After Wallace's sighting, there were no reports of the bee for 123 years. It was assumed to be extinct, but in 1981 American entomologist Adam Messer found six nests of the bee on three islands in the North Moluccas. After that the bee disappeared once again, and it was again feared extinct.

In 2018 three dead specimens emerged—including two that were auctioned on eBay, where they sold for a combined total of more than $13,000. In February 2019 an expedition succeeded in locating the bee in the wild once again.

Wallace wrote that the bee was "about as long as an adult human's thumb," with "immense jaws." He was describing a female, which has a wingspan of 2½ inches (6.3 cm), making it four times larger than a worker honeybee, although the giant bee does not live in large colonies. Males are half the size of females.

Wallace's giant bee is so hard to find because it makes its home inside a termite nest. Females use their jaws to gather balls of tree resin and then build chambers inside the nest. From the outside, the bees' presence in the nest is almost impossible to detect.

LEFT: The original giant bee collected by Alfred Russel Wallace in 1858.

Devil's Hole pupfish

CLASSIFICATION: *Cyprinodon diabolis*
STATUS: Critically endangered
DISTRIBUTION: Death Valley, Nevada
SIZE: 1⅜ in. (3.5 cm) long

The Devil's Hole pupfish is the rarest fish in the world. This scarcity is not due to human activity but instead because its home is one of the most isolated and hostile places in which a fish could possibly find itself.

Devil's Hole is a pool 11 feet 6 inches (3.5 m) wide and 72 feet (22 m) long. That gives the Devil's Hole pupfish the smallest range of any vertebrate. Within the pool, the fish breeds and spawns on a single ledge the size of a large rug.

The pool lies within a cavern in Death Valley, a desert on the border of California and Nevada that is the hottest place on Earth. The water is a bathlike 91.4 degrees Fahrenheit (33°C), hot enough to kill most fish. For two months of the winter, no sunlight falls on the cavern, limiting the growth of the algae that the cavern's animals rely on, and causing the numbers of fish to drop.

Scientists have been making twice-yearly counts of the pupfish since the 1970s. At first the population held steady at several hundred fish. But for unknown reasons it began to decline in the mid-1990s. In 2013 there were only thirty-five fish remaining. Since then the US Fish and Wildlife Service has set up a captive breeding program in a 100,000-gallon (380,000-liter) tank that mimics Devil's Hole. The aim is to maintain a second population that can be reintroduced if disaster strikes in the wild.

The goldfish-size species is the rarest of several pupfish living in isolated pools in Death Valley, which was once far lusher than it is now. It was first thought that the Devil's Hole pupfish were swept into their isolated home in a flood between 10,000 and 20,000 years ago. But in 2016, genetic comparisons showed that it had bred with the other pupfish of Death Valley much more recently. From its DNA, the pupfish appears to have arrived in its cavern just a few hundred years ago—perhaps carried by a bird or a human—and rapidly evolved into a unique species.

ABOVE: The Devil's Hole pupfish lives in an underground pool in the hottest place on Earth.

Horned marsupial frog

CLASSIFICATION: *Gastrotheca cornuta*
STATUS: Endangered
DISTRIBUTION: Costa Rica, Panama, Colombia, Ecuador
SIZE: 3 in. (7.5 cm) long, $^{1}/_{3}$ oz. (10 g)

The horned marsupial frog was first described in 1898 by Belgian zoologist George Albert Boulenger. Following a sighting in 2005, it had been considered extinct in Ecuador until 2018. That year it was rediscovered in the Chocó rain forest in western Ecuador, when a research group of the Tropical Herping initiative heard frog calls they didn't recognize.

The frog is a nocturnal tree dweller that lives high in the rain-forest canopy. Like all marsupial frogs, its eggs develop in a pouch on the back of the female and hatch out fully formed as froglets, without spending any time as free-living tadpoles.

The frog ranges from Ecuador to Costa Rica. Ecuador, however, is losing 2 percent of its rain forest each year. Several other species of marsupial frogs have not been seen for decades. Amphibians worldwide are threatened by such deforestation, as well as climate change and disease.

Ecuador is a hotspot for amphibian biodiversity. Almost 600 species live within the country's borders, nearly half of them found nowhere else, and new species are regularly being discovered. Scientists are working to make the Chocó region a conservation priority to protect its rich diversity and this enigmatic little frog.

OPPOSITE: The horned marsupial frog carries its eggs and young on its back.

RIGHT: The Ecuadoran rain forest is home to hundreds of species of amphibians.

Red colobus

CLASSIFICATION: *Piliocolobus* spp.
STATUS: Endangered and critically endangered
DISTRIBUTION: Africa
SIZE: 3 ft. 3 in. (1 m) long, 17 lb. 8 oz. (8 kg)

More than half of the world's 500 species of primate are threatened with extinction. Logging, farming, and mining are destroying their forest homes. Deforestation also brings roads, which in turn bring hunters and diseases into their habitat.

Every two years, the International Union for Conservation of Nature publishes a list of the twenty-five most endangered species, *Primates in Peril*. The edition for 2018–20 includes five lemurs from Madagascar, orangutans from Indonesia, and six species of monkeys from Latin America. The list also includes two species of red colobus monkeys: the Niger delta red colobus (*Piliocolobus epieni*) and the Tana River red colobus (*Piliocolobus rufomitratus*).

The Niger delta red species lives in marshy forests on the western edge of Africa, where it is under pressure from logging, hunting, and oil drilling. The estimate is that only about 500 individuals remain. The Tana River red colobus lives in Kenya in East Africa, where farming is encroaching on its forest, while dam-building projects are altering its riverside habitat. Just over 1,000 individuals remain. Both species are confined to small fragments of forest.

These are two of eighteen different forms of red colobus living in the forests of sub-Saharan Africa. Most are classed as either endangered or critically endangered, and *Primates in Peril* describes the red colobus as a whole as the most threatened African primate. It does not survive well or breed in captivity.

One species native to the Côte d'Ivoire, Miss Waldron's red colobus (*Piliocolobus waldronae*), has not been seen since 1978. Some still hope that this monkey will be found alive, but in 2000 a fruitless seven-year search concluded that it was probably extinct, making it the first primate species to be lost in 500 years.

LEFT: Miss Waldron's red colobus has not been seen since 1978.

OPPOSITE: Tana River red colobus, one of the world's most endangered primates.

CLASSIFICATION: *Pterodroma cahow*
STATUS: Endangered
DISTRIBUTION: Bermuda
SIZE: 1 ft. 1¾in. (35 cm) long, wingspan 2 ft. 11½ in. (90cm),
9 oz. (250 g)

Bermuda petrel

Before Europeans began to cross the Atlantic, an estimated half a million pairs of petrels nested across the islands of Bermuda, raising their chicks in burrows they dug with their feet and beaks. Even when Spanish ships started to arrive after Columbus's voyage of 1492, the Europeans avoided Bermuda's stormy weather and rocky reefs. Those who landed, however, introduced pigs as food for shipwrecked sailors. The ungulates made short work of the birds' nests, eggs, and chicks.

By the time Bermuda was claimed as a British colony in 1609, the petrels held on in only the most inaccessible parts of the islands. The settlers called the bird the cahow, after its call. The colonists ate the petrels and introduced cats, dogs, and rats that did the same. The last large population, on Cooper's Island, was consumed by settlers fleeing a plague of rats on the main island. Despite the governor issuing a "Proclamation gainst the spoyle and havocke of the cahowes," by 1620 the birds were presumed extinct.

It was a story almost exactly like that of the dodo's, of a species that thrived on a remote island until it was wiped out by Europeans and the animals they brought with them. However, nearly 300 years after it was thought lost, the Bermuda petrel reappeared.

The petrel's habit of spending most of its life hundreds of miles from land and only coming ashore to breed made it elusive. One bird found in 1906 was identified as a Bermuda petrel after comparisons with centuries-old bones. In 1935 another bird died flying into a lighthouse. A live bird was caught and released after flying into a radio antenna in 1941. Finally, in 1951, a party of naturalists found seventeen breeding pairs of Bermuda petrels nesting on four rocky islets in Castle Harbour at the north of the main island.

The rediscovery led to an intensive conservation effort, including the provision of artificial burrows in favorable spots. As of 2019, there were 132 pairs, which produced 72 chicks. Four centuries after the bird was thought lost, webcams now enable us to see inside a Bermuda petrel's burrow from anywhere in the world.

LEFT: The Bermuda petrel was thought extinct for nearly three centuries.

Further Reading

Benton, Michael J., *When Life Nearly Died: The Greatest Mass Extinction of All Time* (Thames & Hudson, 2015)

Brusatte, Steve, *The Rise and Fall of the Dinosaurs: The Untold Story of a Lost World* (Picador, 2018)

Fortey, Richard, *Life: An Unauthorised Biography* (Flamingo, 1998)

Gould, Stephen Jay, *Wonderful Life: Burgess Shale and the Nature of History* (Vintage, 2000)

Kolbert, Elizabeth, *The Sixth Extinction: An Unnatural History* (Bloomsbury, 2014)

Humphrey, Louise and Stringer, Chris, *Our Human Story* (Natural History Museum, 2018)

Knoll, Andrew H, *Life on a Young Planet: The First Three Billion Years of Evolution on Earth* (Princeton University Press, 2015)

Macphee, Ross D. E., *End of the Megafauna: The Fate of the World's Hugest, Fiercest and Strangest Animals* (W. W. Norton, 2018)

Marshall, Michael, 'Timeline: The evolution of life', *New Scientist* https://www.newscientist.com/article/dn17453-timeline-the-evolution-of-life/

Rutherford, Adam, *A Brief History of Everyone Who Ever Lived: The Stories in Our Genes* (Weidenfeld & Nicholson, 2016)

Shapiro, Beth, *How to Clone a Mammoth: The Science of De-extinction* (Princeton University Press, 2016)

Shubin, Neil, *Some Assembly Required: Decoding Four Billion Years of Life, From Ancient Fossils to DNA* (Oneworld, 2020)

Smithsonian National Museum of Natural History, 'What does it mean to be human?' http://humanorigins.si.edu/

Taylor, Paul D. and O'Dea, Aaron, *A History of Life in 100 Fossils* (Natural History Museum, 2014)

Thomas, Chris D., *Inheritors of the Earth: How Nature is Thriving in an Age of Extinction* (Penguin, 2017)

Walker, Gabrielle, *Snowball Earth: The Story of the Great Global Catastrophe that Spawned Life As We Know It* (Bloomsbury, 2004)

Zimmer, Carl, *At the Water's Edge: Fish with Fingers, Whales with Legs and How Life Came Shore but Then Went Back to the Sea* (Touchstone, 1999)

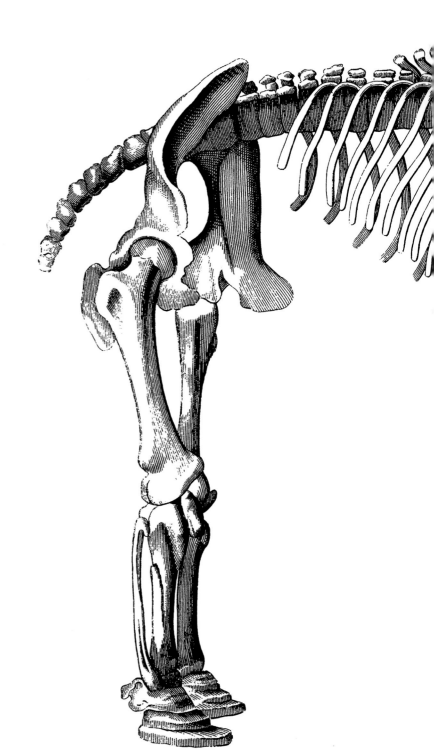

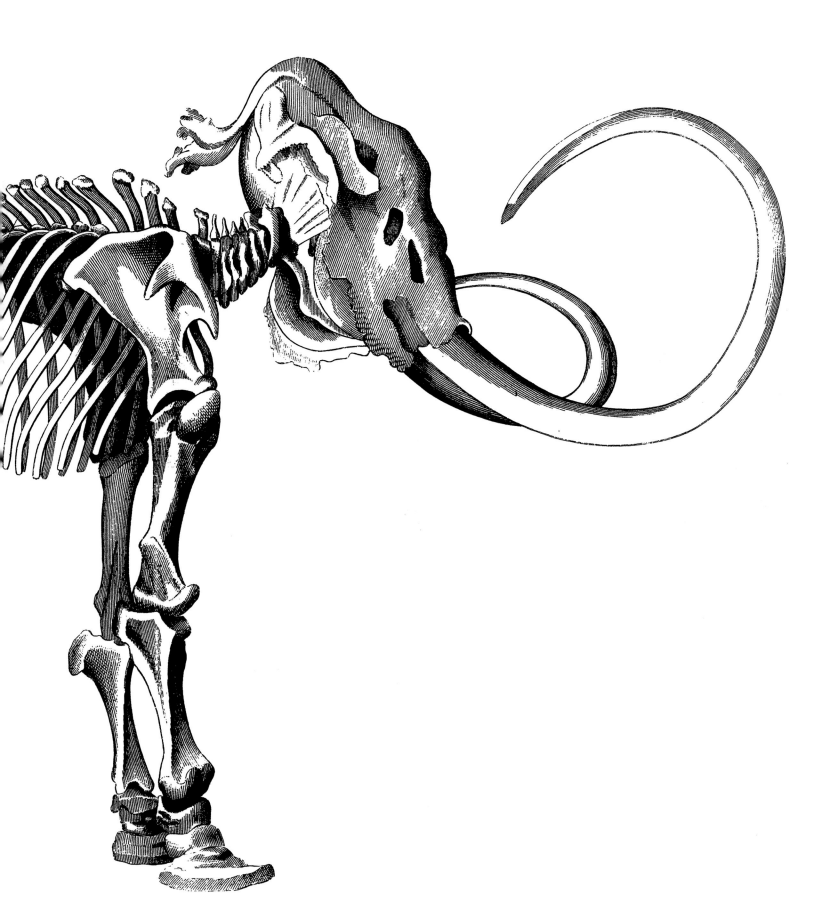

Picture Credits

The publishers would like to thank the following sources for their kind permission to reproduce the pictures in this book.

Key: t = top, b = bottom, c = center, l = left, and r = right

AKG–Images: Liszt Collection 126l; /World History Archive 91

Alamy: 58–59; /Agefotostock 72, 84t; /Arco Images GmbH 203; /Balfore Archive Images 191; /Biosphoto 204; /Florillegius 10; /All Canada Photos 57; /Richard Bizley 50; /Sabena Jane Blackbird 21, 129, 157; /John Canacalosi 48–49, 202; /Chase Studio 30; /Chris Stock Photography 107; /Corbin17 51b, 60, 97; /Dorling Kindersley Ltd: 74–75; /Dotted Zebra 28–29, 40, 42–43, 180–181; /Mohamad Haghani 108–109; /Kerry Hargrove 209; /Chris Hellier 199t; /Hemis 194–195; /Puwadol Jaturawutthuchai 154; /Sebastian Kaulitzki 36; /National Geographic Image Collection 148; /Natural History Museum 29t, 37, 51t, 62b, 65t, 69, 78, 82, 99, 100t, 100b, 177, 210; /Nature Photographers Ltd: 216–217; /Nature Picture Library 19, 186, 215; /Boyd Norton 153; /The Picture Art Collection 185; /Prisma Archivo 110t; /PvE 155; /Morley Read 213; /Science Photo Library 41, 92–93, 98; /Paul D Stewart 192; /Stocktrek Images 84b; /Stone Nature Photography 211; /Vaccaro Paolo 34; /Dave Watts 200–201; /Cathy Withers-Clarke 12–13; /World History Archive 198, 199b; /YG-Travel-Photo 205; /Zoonar GmbH 26–27

American Museum of Natural History: 168

Lutz Benseler: 73

Zhiduan Chen: 81b

DK Images: 53

Getty Images: Buyenlarge 89; /Matt Cardy 89t; /Corey Ford/StockTrek Images 33; /De Agostini 80; /Daniel Eskridge 176; /Raphael Gaillarde/Gamma-Rapho 169t; /Mark Garlick 66–67; /Insights/Universal Images Group 141; /Istock 44; /Tony Karumba/AFP 187; /Bill O'Leary/The Washington Post 106; /Schellhorn/ullstein bild 169b; /Schöning/ullstein bild 94; /SSPL 182; /Universal History Archive/Universal Images 76, 218–219; /Group Wild Horizons/Universal Images Group 6–7; /Bernard Weil/Toronto Star 103; /John Weinstein/Field Museum Library 79

Brian Gratwicke: 212

Anton Handlirsch: 52

Aleksey Nagovitsyn: 24

Copyright 2019 the Author(s). Published by PNAS. This open access article is distributed under Creative Commons Attribution License 4.0 (CC BY). National Academy of Sciences/Bo Wang: 105

Private Collection: 197

Science Photo Library: Maurico Anton 83, 142–143, 164, 170–171; /Des Bartlett 162r; /Prof Matthew Bennett, Bournemouth University 164; /Biophoto Associates 54; /Richard Bizley 71t; /Leonello Calvetti 95, 110b, 114–115; /Jaime Chirinos 86–87, 190; /Collection Abecasis 55; /Jullius T Csotonyi 102, 111; /Christian Darkin 140; /De Agostini/UIG 116, 132; /Phil Degginger 4; /Dorling Kindersley/UIG 112; /S.Entressangle/E.Daynes 160, 167, 178; /Ikelos GMBH/Dr. Christopher B. Jackson 23b; /Kennis & Kennis 159; /Patrick Landmann 150; /Michael Long 85, 118, 133t, 146; /Walter Myers 47, 104, 119; /National Geographic Society 162l; /Natural History Museum, London 80, 81t, 88, 130–131, 151, 152, 165, 196; /National Science Foundation 61; /Philippe Plaily 158; /John Reader 156, 161t, 161b; /Millard H. Sharp/Science Source 3, 126, 139t, 174; /Martin Shields/Science Source 137; /John Sibbick 14, 32, 63, 68, 96, 128, 221; /Alan Sirulnikoff 18; /Philippe Plailly 172; /Sputnik 11, 133b; /Sinclair Stammers 22, 25, 31, 35; /Volker Steger 179; /Paul D Stewart 120–121; /Barbara Strnadova 163; /Stocktrek Images, Inc. 64–65; /Simon Terrey 17; /Javier Trueba/MSF 173; /Joe Tucciarone 113; /Mark Turner 175; /Victor Habbick Visions 136; /QA International 62t; /Dirk Wiersma 48

Shutterstock: 188–189; /Auscape/UIG 20; /Conservation Int 214; /Peter Foley/EPA 101; /Fulcanelli 206–207; /Richard Jones 208; /Nielsdk/imageBROKER 193; /Brian Skoloff/AP 184

Martin R. Smith: 38–39

Fred Spoor: 145

Matteo De Stefano/MUSE: 56

© Roman Uchytel: 122, 123, 124–125, 127, 134–135, 138–139, 144, 147

Zongjun Yin/National Academy of Sciences: 23t

Illustrations and maps on pages 9, 16, 46, and 80 by Geoff Borin

Every effort has been made to acknowledge correctly and contact the source and/or copyright holder of each picture and Welbeck Publishing apologizes for any unintentional errors or omissions, which will be corrected in future editions of this book.

PICTURE CREDITS

Index

INDEX